F is for football

A COLLECTION OF ANECDOTES, QUOTES AND FOOTBALLING STORIES WITH A FOREWORD BY BOB 'THE CAT' BEVAN.

Compiled and Written by Vanessa Gardner

F is for football

This edition first published in the UK in 2005
By Green Umbrella
www.greenumbrella.co.uk

© Green Umbrella Publishing 2005

Publishers Jules Gammond, Tim Exell

Printed and bound in China.

ISBN 1-905009-070

The views in this book are those of the author but they are general views only and readers are urged to consult the relevant and qualified specialist for individual advice in particular situations.

Green Umbrella Sport and Leisure hereby exclude all liability to the extent permitted by law of any errors or omissions in this book and for any loss, damage or expense (whether direct or indirect) suffered by a third party relying on any information supplied in this book.

All our best endeavours have been made to secure copyright clearance for every photograph used but in the event of any copyright owner being overlooked please address correspondence to Green Umbrella Sport and Leisure, Old Woking Road, Old Woking, Surrey, GU22 8BF

Contents

Foreword
Bob 'the Cat' Bevan

Bob "the Cat" Bevan MBE was described by Sir Bobby Robson as the funniest person he has heard on football "in all my experience." He has been entertaining audiences since his early days as a midfielder and most famously, a goalkeeper since the 1960s. His book, "Nearly Famous" was described by the Daily Mail as "having more laughs than a dozen sports autobiographies".

My first memory of football was 1954. I watched the FA Cup Final between West Bromwich Albion and Preston North End on the black and white TV my grandmother had bought for the Coronation the year before. On the same set I watched some kid called Greaves rattling in goals in Youth Internationals. He is still my hero and today, we are friends as well.

I have no time for those who moan that the game isn't what it was; that there are no characters around. I love the game today as much as I ever did.

I like nearly everyone I've met in football and I still look forward to watching the next game as much as I did back in the 1950s.

Sport is a force for good — something no UK Government has ever grasped — and football is part of that. I don't care if they get paid big money. I know that most of these top players love the game as much as I do. I'm utterly convinced that David Beckham would play for nothing. You can see he just loves to play. Like most top players he is a great entertainer. Why do we never read complaints in the press about pop stars or actors being highly paid? Added to which their careers can last a good deal longer than a footballer.

When I'm not watching Crystal Palace I can occasionally be found at Tonbridge Angels FC and even less occasionally at my first football love, Dulwich Hamlet.

Just as rarely will I go to Old Wilsonians FC where I played for 25 years. It was here that the greatest humour was to be found. One of my favourites was a report in the weekly newsletter. The 3rd XI had just played on a very icy pitch and one of the players, Brian Stapleton, wrote, "the pitch was so slippery we had a job to turn round at half-time."

At non-league grounds the spectators still change ends at half-time swapping banter with the opposition fans as they go.

This is what football and sport is all about – fierce rivalry of course, but equally, respect for the opposition and having a laugh; having some fun.

If that's what you're looking for then you've definitely bought the right book.

BOB 'THE CAT' BEVAN

THE PUNDITS

Football punditry is an art of sorts, and with every football pundit there are the inevitable gaffes as well as the occasional words of wisdom.

This chapter brings you a selection of classic punditry that has been collated from decades of football coverage both on the radio and the television.

Every football fan has a favourite football commentator. The arguments about John Motson versus Brian Moore in the eighties were ever apparent, particularly in the run up to a World Cup or European tournament. Often our decision to watch BBC, or ITV, or SKY is determined by our personal views about a particular commentator.

Commentators are a mixed breed. Some come from a journalistic or broadcasting background, while for others commentating is their career, and then there are the ex-footballers and ex-football managers who think it's their god-given right to irritate the hell out of us with their ridiculous opinions!

Love them or hate them, but mostly we can laugh at them!

This chapter is a tribute to those who have given us the funniest quotes in football, and to those who continue to plague us on a regular basis.
They are heroes of the microphone, who don't put their brains into gear before they speak.

Long may they reign!

"I KNOW WHERE HE SHOULD HAVE PUT HIS FLAG UP, AND HE'D HAVE GOT PLENTY OF HELP."

John Motson...

BELOW Motson at home rehearsing his matchday commentary.

"For those of you watching in black and white, Spurs are in the all yellow strip."

"I think this could be our best victory over Germany since the war."

"In a sense it's a one-man show... except there are two men involved, Hartson and Berkovic, and a third man, the goalkeeper."

"And I suppose they (Spurs) are nearer to being out of the FA Cup now than at any other time since the first half of this season, when they weren't ever in it anyway."

"I can confirm that Trevor Brooking did have his own eggs and bacon before setting off this morning."
– Motty's breakfast obsession continues.

"Not the first half you might have expected, even though the score might suggest that it was."

"The match has become quite unpredictable, but it still looks as though Arsenal will win the cup."

"Hold onto the cups and glasses at home... you can smash them now! David Beckham has scored for England!"

"There is still nothing on the proverbial scoreboard."

"And Seaman, just like a falling oak, manages to change direction."

"That shot might not have been as good as it might have been."

❝You couldn't count the number of moves Alan Ball made... I counted four and possibly five.❞

❝...so different from the scenes in 1872, at the Cup Final that none of us can remember.❞

❝I was about to say, before something far more interesting interrupted.❞

❝You can have your breakfast with Batistuta and your cornflakes with Crespo.❞

❝This is a once-in-a-lifetime opportunity for these players. Well, twice in a lifetime if you count the first match.❞

❝The World Cup is a truly International event.❞

ABOVE "Bruce has got the taste of Wembley in his nostrils."

❝Nearly all the Brazilian supporters are wearing yellow shirts – it's a fabulous kaleidoscope of colour!❞

❝Northern Ireland were in white, which was quite appropriate because three inches of snow had to be cleared from the pitch before kick-off.❞

❝The referee is wearing the same yellow-coloured top as the Slovakian goalkeeper. I'd have thought the UEFA official would have spotted that – but perhaps he's been deafened by the noise of this crowd.❞

❝Oh, that's good running on the run.❞

❝The match has become quite unpredictable, but it still looks as though Arsenal will win the cup.❞

❝The goals made such a difference to the way this game went.❞

Brian Moore...

BELOW "Bryan Robson wears his shirt on his sleeve."

"And their manager, Terry Neil, isn't here today, which suggests he is elsewhere."

"History, as John Boyd would agree, is all about toadies and not about yesterdays."

"Wilkins, with an inch perfect pass to no one in particular."

"...and the news from Guadalajara where the temperature is 96 degrees, is that Falcao is warming up."

"Mark Hughes. Sparky by name, Sparky by nature. The same can be said of Brian McClair."

"Everybody thought the Saudis were coming here as chopping blocks."

"Alongside me is Keggy Keegle – sorry, Kevin Keegle..."

"This is going to be a very long 30 minutes with 26 minutes left."

"Adams is stretching himself, looking for Seaman."

"He has always played for Inter Milan, whilst his brother plays just across the city at AC Milan, who of course share the same stadium."

"Newcastle, of course, unbeaten in their last five wins."

"And now the familiar site of Liverpool raising the League Cup for the first time."

Trevor Brooking...

"Merseyside derbies usually last 90 minutes and I'm sure today's won't be any different."

"That's football, Mike, Northern Ireland have had several chances and haven't scored but England have had no chances and scored twice."

Lineker: "Trevor Brooking is in the Sapporo Bowl. What's it like, Trevor?"
Brooking: "Well, it's a bowl shape, Gary."

"Unfortunately, we don't get a second chance. We've already played them twice."

"Poor Miklosko. Hasn't had to make a save, yet he's let three goals in!"

BELOW "Martin Keown is up everybody's backsides."

"The crowd not surprisingly standing on their feet."

"Historically, the host nations do well in Euro 2000."

"Fortunately, Paul Scholes's injury wasn't as bad as we'd hoped for."

"Being naturally right-footed he doesn't often chance his arm with his left foot."

"It's end to end stuff, but from side to side."

"Many clubs have a question mark in the shape of an axe-head hanging over them."

Kevin Keegan...

BELOW Keegan — when perms were still in fashion.

❝That decision for me, was almost certainly wrong.❞

❝I tell Laurent (Charvet): 'Ey, there's no reason why you can't take your training out on to the big pitch here.' I keep telling him 'Tres Bien' all the time, whatever that means.❞

❝My father was a miner and he worked down a mine.❞

❝They compare Steve McManaman to Steve Heighway and he's nothing like him, but I can see why — it's because he's a bit different.❞

❝The good news for Nigeria is that they're two-nil down very early in the game.❞

❝The Ref was vertically 15 yards away.❞

❝Chile have three options — they could win or they could lose.❞

❝We have spent three matches chasing a football.❞

❝The substitute is about to come on — he's a player who was left out of the starting line-up today.❞

❝I'll never play at Wembley again, unless I play at Wembley again.❞

❝At the Argentina game, how would you have guessed that Darren Anderton would have gone off with cramp?❞

❝England have the best fans in the world and Scotland's fans are second to none.❞

"After a goalless first half, the score at half-time is 0-0."

"In some ways, cramp is worse than having a broken leg."

"They're the second best team in the world, and there's no higher praise than that."

"The 33- or 34-year-olds will be 36 or 37 by the time the next World Cup comes around, if they're not careful."

"Nicolas Anelka left Arsenal for £23 million and they built a training ground on him."

"I'm not disappointed – just disappointed."

"Danny Tiatto is not going to make a mistake on purpose."

ABOVE "I don't think there's anyone bigger or smaller than Maradona."

"You get bunches of players like you do bananas, though that is a bad comparison."

"Despite his white boots, he has pace and aggression."

"It's understandable that people are keeping one eye on the pot and another up the chimney."

"Argentina won't be at Euro 2000 because they're from South America."

"The tide is very much in our court now."

"Goalkeepers aren't born today until they're in their late twenties or thirties."

"The Germans only have one player under 22, and he's 23."

Ron Atkinson...

"There's nobody fitter at his age, except maybe Raquel Welch."
– Ron Atkinson lauds Gordon Strachan, 39.

"I know where he should have put his flag up, and he'd have got plenty of help."

"There's not a lot of demand for a non-scoring striker."

"They've certainly grown, the Japanese. I mean grown in stature, playing-wise."

"He's not only a good player, but he's spiteful in the nicest sense of the word."

"Diouf has a lot of lone ranging to do tonight."

"The lad throws it further than I go on holiday."

BELOW 'Big Ron' having a bad day at the office.

"They only thought the shirts had to go out to get a win."

"Moreno thought that the full back was gonna come up behind and give him one really hard."

"Someone in the England team will have to grab the ball by the horns."

"Ryan Giggs is running long up the backside."

"I would not say David Ginola is the best left winger in the Premiership, but there are none better."

"Well, Clive, it's all about the two M's. Movement and positioning."

"Zero-zero is a big score."

"The keeper was unsighted – he still didn't see it."

"I've had this sneaking feeling throughout the game that it's there to be won…"

"Suker – first touch like a camel."

"He sliced the ball when he had it on a plate."

"I'm afraid they've left their legs at home."

"He must be lightning slow."

"Now Manchester United are 2-1 down on aggregate, they are in a better position than when they started the game at 1-1."

ABOVE "Carlton Palmer can trap the ball further than I can kick it."

"They've done the old-fashioned things well; they've kicked the ball, they've headed it."

"Beckenbauer really has gambled all his eggs."

"They've picked their heads up off the ground and they now have a lot to carry on their shoulders."

"On another night, they'd have won 2-2."

"I think that was a moment of cool panic there."

"I never comment on referees and I'm not going to break the habit of a lifetime for that prat."

"Well, either side could win it, or it could be a draw."

Gary Lineker...

❝Ronaldo: The man who could eat an apple through a tennis racket.❞

❝The World Cup is every four years, so it's going to be a perennial problem.❞

❝It was more fight club than football club, and the usual suspects!❞ – On Kieron Dyer and Lee Bowyer's punch up in front of 50,000 fans

❝Things looking desperate for the French. Could it be time for Zidane? Zi-Desperate-Dan!❞

❝Of Course everyone has a chance of winning the World Cup but in England's case it looks a slim chance. We might have to beat France, Brazil and Argentina just to reach the final. We will need a huge slice of fortune.❞

BELOW "... an excellent player, but he (Ian Wright) does have a black side."

❝Every team could finish on six in this group!❞ – Lineker displays his impressive mathematical abilities.

❝He's got a lot of forehead.❞ – Speaking of Sven Goran Eriksson.

❝To be honest, it would have been better to watch it on Ceefax.❞ – Lineker comments on a Wimbledon game.

❝Most of the players will be wearing rubbers tonight.❞

❝There's no in-between – you're either good or bad. We were in-between.❞

Best of the Rest...

"An inch or two either side of the post and that would have been a goal."
– Dave Bassett

"Every time they attacked we were memorised by them." – Charlie Nicholas

"Martin O'Neill, standing, hands on hips, stroking his chin." – Mike Ingham

"Julian Dicks is everywhere. It's like they've got eleven Dicks on the field."
– Metro Radio

"Craig Bellamy has literally been on fire."
– Ally McCoist

"The referee was booking everyone. I thought he was filling in his lottery numbers." – Ian Wright

"I'd be surprised if all 22 players are on the field at the end of the game – one has already been sent off." – George Best

"For such a small man, Maradona gets great elevation on his balls." – David Pleat

"Once Tony Daley opens his legs, you've got a problem."
– Howard Wilkinson

"The Belgians will play like their fellow Scandinavians, Denmark and Sweden." – Andy Townsend

"Glen Hoddle hasn't been the Hoddle we know. Neither has Bryan Robson."
– Ron Greenwood

"That was only a yard away from being an inch perfect pass." – Murdo MacLeod

BELOW David Pleat.

ABOVE "The ageless Dennis Wise, now in his thirties." – Martin Tyler.

Best of the Rest...

"I was saying the other day, how often the most vulnerable area for goalies is between their legs..." — Andy Gray

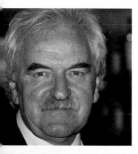

BELOW Des Lynam.

"The Italians are hoping for an Italian victory." — David Coleman

"This will be their nineteenth consecutive game without a win unless they can get an equaliser." — Alan Green

"More football later, but first let's see the goals from the Scottish Cup final." — Des Lynam

"Neil Sullivan has stopped absolutely everything thrown at him ...Wimbledon 1, Manchester United 1." — Mike Ingham

"Mick McCarthy will have to replace Cascarino because he's quickly running out of legs." — Mark Lawrenson

ABOVE "Despite the rain, it's still raining here at Old Trafford." — Jimmy Hill

Jimmy Hill: "Don't sit on the fence Terry, what chance do you think Germany has got of getting through?" Terry Venables: "I think it's fifty – fifty."

"You can't win anything with kids." — Alan Hansen comments on Manchester United's 3–1 opening-day defeat by Aston Villa. Who won the league that year? Man Utd went on to win.

"It took a lot of bottle for Tony (Adams) to own up." — Ian Wright on the Arsenal captain's confession to alcoholism.

"Viv Anderson has passed a fatness test." — John Helm

❝I hate to speak poorly of them (Man City) but... they are crap.❞ – Rodney Marsh

❝It's now 1–1, an exact reversal of the score on Saturday.❞ – Radio 5 Live

❝I'm not convinced that Scotland will play a typically English game.❞
– Gareth Southgate

❝I wouldn't trust Newcastle's back five to protect my garden gnomes from squirrels.❞
– Jonathan Pearce, as Newcastle are beaten in the FA Cup by Wolves 3–2.

❝As the old-timers say, 'Don't rub 'em, count 'em.'❞ – Joe Royle, on an eye-watering moment for South Korea's Lee Eul Young

❝If Jurgen Klinsmann was still playing he'd have been skint by the end of the month.❞
– Andy Townsend on FIFA's new set of fines for divers.

❝They're in pole position, i.e. in 3rd position, for the Champions League.❞ –
Mark Lawrenson

❝Sporting Lisbon in their green and white hoops, looking like a team of zebras.❞
– Peter Jones

❝Manchester United are looking to Frank Stapleton to pull some magic out of the fire.❞ – Jimmy Hill

❝Some of these players never dreamed they would be playing in a Cup Final at Wembley, and now here they are fulfilling those dreams.❞
– Lawrie McMenemy

BELOW Jonathan Pearce.

ABOVE "Djorkaeff will be playing in Zidane's hole." – Clive Tyldesley

Best of the Rest...

"Nicky Butt, he's another aptly named player. He joins things, brings one sentence to an end and starts another.**"** – Barry Davies

BELOW Barry Davies.

"Izzet – no is the answer.**"** – Barry Davies

"The eyes said 'yes'. The woodwork said 'no'.**"** – Clive Tyldsley

"Tottenham are trying tonight to become the first London team to win this Cup. The last team to do so was the 1973 Spurs side.**"** – Mike Ingham

"The crowd think that Todd handled the ball... they must have seen something that nobody else did.**"** – Barry Davies

"He hit that one like an arrow.**"** – Alan Parry

"Korsten is making a meal of it... er... that's clearly a penalty, yes.**"** – Trevor Francis

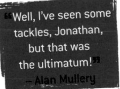

"Well, I've seen some tackles, Jonathan, but that was the ultimatum!**"** – Alan Mullery

"All the cul-de-sacs are closed for Scotland.**"** – Joe Jordan

"It's imperable that they get off to a good start.**"** – Charlie Nicholas

"It's real end-to-end stuff, but unfortunately it's all up at Forest's end.**"** – Chris Kamara

ABOVE "Roy Keane, his face punches the air..." – Alan Brazil

"It's like a big Christmas pudding out there.**"** – Don Howe

"And for those of you watching without television sets, live commentary is on Radio 2." – David Coleman

"One thing about Germany – they'll be organised, they'll be big, and they'll be strong." – Ally McCoist

BELOW Mark Lawrenson.

"The Swedish back four is amongst the tallest in the world cup. Their average age is 7 foot 4." – Chris Waddle

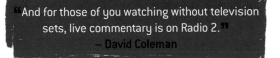

Rob McLean: "John Hartson is playing superbly today." Sandy Clark: "Yes, Rob, there's no one better today." McLean: "So, Sandy, who is your man of the match?" Clark: "Alan Thompson."

"Xavier, who looks just like Zeus, not that I have any idea what Zeus looks like..." – Alan Green

"McCarthy shakes his head in agreement with the referee." – Martin Tyler

"... a tale of too many cooks in the defence." – Ian Brown

"It's slightly alarming the way Manchester United decapitated against Stuttgart" – Mark Lawrenson

"He signals to the bench with his groin." – Mark Bright

"It's been 17 years since Celtic first won this competition, and after tonight it could be 18." – Roddy Forsyth

"Bristol Rovers were 4–0 up at half time, with four goals in the first half." – Tony Adamson

ABOVE "Solskjaer never misses the target. That time he hit the post." – Peter Schmeichel

Best of the Rest...

John Sinclair: **"**Will Steve Agnew take this free kick just outside the box?**"** Steve Agnew: **"**I'm sitting next to you, so I don't think it'll be me.**"**

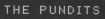

BELOW Martin Tyler.

"Giggs drops deep into that Sheringham position where he can turn and ride defenders.**"** – Martin Tyler

"Paul Scholes with four players in front of him – five if you count Gary Neville.**"** – Darragh Moloney

"A smoked salmon sandwich of a football match if ever there has been one.**"** – Peter Drury

"Football today would certainly not be the same if it had never existed.**"** – Elton Welsby

"If it comes to penalties – one of these two great sides could go out on the whim of a ball.**"** – Peter Shreeve

"Not being in the Rumbelows Cup for those teams won't mean a row of beans, 'cos that's only small potatoes.**"** – Ian St. John

"Chris Waddle is off the field at the moment; exactly the position he is at his most menacing.**"** – Gerald Sinstad

ABOVE "Ardiles strokes the ball like it was part of his anatomy." – Jimmy Magee

"...and tonight we have the added ingredient of Kenny Dalglish not being here.**"** – Martin Tyler

"When you think about it, there's three games per working week - Saturday, mid-week and Saturday again.**"** – Jimmy Greaves

"The Liverpool players are passing the cup down the line like a new born baby. Although when they are back in the dressing room they will probably fill it with champagne, something you should never do to a baby." – Alan Parry

"I've seen some players with very big feet, and some with very small feet." – David Pleat

"Poborsky's had one or two moments – two, actually." – Des Lynam

"Hagi has got a left foot like Brian Lara's bat." – Don Howe

"Walter Smith has come down from the directors box to tinkle with his tactical formation." – Jock Brown

"Its an incredible rise to stardom, at 17 you're more likely to get a call from Michael Jackson than Sven Goran Eriksson." – Gordon Strachan on Wayne Rooney

"The one thing England have got is spirit, resolve, grit and determination." – Alan Hansen

"Emmanuel Petit has won more medals than any other player in the Premiership this year, although Patrick Vieira's won the same medals." – Brian Woolnough

"Lukic saved with his foot, which is all part of the goalkeeper's arm" – Barry Davies

"Some teams are so negative, they could have been sponsored by Kodak." – Tommy Docherty

ABOVE "By the look of him he must have headed a lot of balls." Harry Redknapp about the lovely Iain Dowie

"It's one of the greatest goals ever, but I'm surprised that people are talking about it being the goal of the season." – Andy Gray

"XAVIER, WHO LOOKS JUST LIKE ZEUS, NOT THAT I HAVE ANY IDEA WHAT ZEUS LOOKS LIKE..."
— ALAN GREEN

PRE-MATCH PEP TALK

KIT BAG

THE MANAGEMENT

Managers are a law unto themselves. They have excuses for every occasion. Some even make sense, most though are just plain ridiculous!

This chapter demonstrates the eloquence of some of the world's finest managers, who with dogged determination believe they have the best team on the pitch even when they lose.

Excuses abound, with support and loyalty for players triumphant, often beyond all reason. Managers have different styles; from the politeness and occasional myopia of Arsene Wenger, to the stinging repartee of the late, great Brian Clough.

Included in this chapter are some of the best quotes to have crossed the lips of football legends such as Sir Alf Ramsey, Bill Shankly, Bob Paisley, Sir Alex Ferguson, and Brian Clough. We also sample the infinite wisdom of some of the lower league managers, whose main occupation it often seems is trying to hold on to their jobs.

Football management — the only job where it's important not to stare the facts in the face!

"WE HAVE PEOPLE COMING HERE TO ADMIRE THE SCENERY AND ENJOY THEIR CRISPS."

Alex Ferguson...

"The lads really ran their socks into the ground."

"When the Italians tell you it's pasta on the plate I even check under the sauce to make sure it really is."

"The philosophy of a lot of European teams, even in home matches, is not to give a goal away."

"I can still remember my very first game in charge away at Oxford. I had done my team-talk and was going into the dugout when I saw the bus driver sitting there. He was even giving the tea out at half time. Let's say that quickly stopped."

"Their effort was obscene." – After relegated West Ham had the audacity to beat United and wreck their 1992 title challenge.

BELOW 'Fergie' directing operations from the touchline.

"Big? It isn't big. It's magnificent! I've seen some whoppers in my time, but Dion's is something else." – his verdict on Dion Dublin's lunchbox, according to the then Coventry chairman Bryan Richardson, in 1994.

"I f*****g told yese not to ask that John. You know the rules here." – To John Motson after Motty had the cheek to ask why Roy Keane had slugged Jan Fjortoft in 1995.

"It's a conflict of parallels."

"This pilot move by FIFA will take root and fly."

"We have people coming here to admire the scenery and enjoy their crisps."

"He probably started crying."
— Explaining why Jack Walker would not let Alan Shearer go to Old Trafford in 1996.

"It's interesting that the games in which we've dropped points are those where we've failed to score." — Amazing!

"Clubs come away from Anfield choking on their own vomit and biting their own tongues knowing they have been done by the referee."
— Airing his love of Liverpool Football Club for the first time after ten-man United grabbed a 3-3 draw in 1988.

ABOVE "Cole should be scoring from those distances, but I'm not going to single him out."

"If he was an inch taller he'd be the best centre half in Britain. His father is 6ft 2in — I'd check the milkman." — Discussing Gary Neville's parentage in 1996.

"This is the greatest moment of my life and I'm struggling to take it in. I haven't said anything to my players yet. I've just hugged and kissed them. I've slobbered over them" — On winning the treble in 1999.

"He used to play tapes of Bill Shankly talking. I remember that and a singer he liked. I don't know who it was but it was crap. He played it on the team bus too and all the boys hated it. Until one night it got chucked away. If he's still wondering who threw that tape off the bus, it was me. So maybe he was right and I'm not to be trusted."
— Gordon Strachan on Sir Alex Ferguson.

"I can't believe it. I can't believe it. Football. Bloody hell."
— Alex Ferguson after Manchester United stunned Bayern Munich with two injury time goals to win 2–1 in the 1999 European Champions League Final.

"He's a bully, a f*****g big-time Charlie."
— Warm praise for his former midfield stalwart Paul Ince in 1998.

Brian Clough...

"I wouldn't say I was the best manager in the business. But I was in the top one."

"Anybody who can do anything in Leicester but make a jumper has got to be a genius." – A tribute to Martin O'Neill.

"On occasions I have been big headed. I think most people are when they get in the limelight. I call myself Big Head just to remind myself not to be." – Old Big 'Ead explains his nickname.

"Man U in Brazil? I hope they get bloody diarrhoea." – On Manchester United opting out of the FA Cup for World Club Championships.

"I bet their dressing room will smell of garlic rather than liniment over the next few months." – On the number of French players at Arsenal.

BELOW 'Cloughie' and his old mate Peter Taylor.

"If God wanted us to play football in the air, then he would have built a pitch in the clouds."

"The ugliest player I ever signed was Kenny Burns." – A compliment to Kenny Burns.

"That Seaman is a handsome young man but he spends too much time looking in his mirror rather than at the ball. You can't keep goal with hair like that."

"I can't even spell spaghetti, never mind talk Italian. How could I tell an Italian to get the ball? He might grab mine." – On the influx of foreign players.

"I want no epitaphs of profound history and all that type of thing. I contributed. I would hope they would say that, and I would hope somebody liked me." – On being remembered.

"I'm sure the England selectors thought if they took me on and gave me the job, I'd want to run the show. They were shrewd because that's exactly what I would have done." — **On not getting the England manager's job.**

ABOVE "I'd have cut his balls off." — On Eric Cantona's infamous kung fu kick at a fan.

"I only ever hit Roy the once. He got up so I couldn't have hit him very hard." — **On dealing with Roy Keane.**

"He should guide Posh in the direction of a singing coach because she's nowhere near as good at her job as her husband." — **On David Beckham.**

"Walk on water? I know most people out there will be saying that instead of walking on it, I should have taken more of it with my drinks. They are absolutely right." — On his alcohol problem.

"I am a big-head not a figurehead."

"The Derby players have seen more of his balls than the one they're meant to be playing with." — **On the streaker who appeared during Derby's game against Manchester United.**

"We used to go to the pictures every Saturday night but we had to leave a little bit early and get home and watch Match of the Day — and my wife still complains she missed the last five minutes of every film we saw." — **On 40 years of Match of the Day.**

"They say Rome wasn't built in a day, but I wasn't on that particular job." — **On his self-belief.**

"We talk about it for 20 minutes and then we decide I was right." — **On dealing with players who disagree.**

"I've been off the booze for more than six months now — doctor's orders. If I ever go back to the bottle, Eriksson will get the blame."

Bill Shankly...

BELOW To his players after failing to sign Lou Macari: **"I only wanted him for the reserves."**

❝Some people believe football is a matter of life and death; I am very disappointed with that attitude. I can assure you it is much, much more important than that.❞

❝Football is a simple game based on the giving and taking of passes, of controlling the ball and of making yourself available to receive a pass. It is terribly simple.❞

❝If Everton were playing at the bottom of the garden, I'd pull the curtains.❞

❝Fire in your belly comes from pride and passion in wearing the red shirt. We don't need to motivate players because each of them is responsible for the performance of the team as a whole. The status of Liverpool's players keeps them motivated.❞

To a Liverpool fan: ❝Where are you from?❞ ❝I'm a Liverpool fan from London.❞ ❝Well laddie... what's it like to be in heaven?❞

❝A million wouldn't buy him, and I'd be one of them.❞

❝Of course I didn't take my wife to see Rochdale as an anniversary present. It was her birthday. Would I have got married in the football season? Anyway, it was Rochdale reserves.❞

❝I'm just one of the people who stands on the kop. They think the same as I do, and I think the same as they do. It's a kind of marriage of people who like each other.❞

❝Son, you'll do well here as long as you remember two things. Don't over-eat and don't lose your accent.❞
– On the day he signed Ian St. John.

"Take that bandage off. And what do you mean about YOUR knee? It's Liverpool's knee!" – To Tommy Smith, who tried to explain that his bandaged knee was injured.

"Aye, here we are with problems at the top of the league." – To the journalist suggesting Liverpool were in difficulties.

"He's worse than the rain in Manchester. At least the rain in Manchester stops occasionally." – On Brian Clough.

To a barber, when asked if he wanted anything off the top: "Aye, Everton."

A scout told Shankly about a young player he'd given a trial to at Liverpool: "He has football in his blood" the scout said. "You may be right," Shankly said, "but it hasn't reached his legs yet!"

ABOVE "Just go out and drop a few hand grenades all over the place, son." – To Kevin Keegan.

"Don't worry, Alan. At least you'll be able to play close to a great team!" – To Alan Ball, who'd just signed for Everton.

"Just tell them I completely disagree with everything they say!" – To a translator, when surrounded by gesticulating Italian journalists.

"You son, you could start a riot in a graveyard." – To Tommy Smith.

At Dixie Dean's funeral: "I know this is a sad occasion but I think that Dixie would be amazed to know that even in death he could draw a bigger crowd than Everton can on a Saturday afternoon."

Talking to a Liverpool trainee: "The problem with you, son, is that all your brains are in your head."

National Team Managers
Bobby Robson...

> ❝Well, we got nine and you can't score more than that.❞

> ❝Their football was exceptionally good – and they played some good football.❞

> ❝I'm not going to look beyond the semi-final – but I would love to lead Newcastle out at the final.❞

> ❝In a year's time, he's a year older.❞

> ❝Eighteen months ago they (Sweden) were arguably one of the best three teams in Europe, and that would include Germany, Holland, Russia and anybody else if you like.❞

> ❝If we start counting our chickens before they hatch, they won't lay any eggs in the basket.❞

> ❝I thought that individually and as a pair, they'd do better together.❞

BELOW "Denis Law once kicked me at Wembley in front of the Queen in an International. I mean, no man is entitled to do that, really."

> ❝Where do you get an experienced player like him with a left foot and a head?❞

> ❝Tottenham have impressed me: they haven't thrown in the towel even though they have been under the gun.❞

> ❝I played cricket for my local village. It was 40 overs per side, and the team that had the most runs won. It was that sort of football.❞

> ❝We didn't underestimate them. They were a lot better than we thought.❞

> ❝He's got his legs back, of course, or his leg – he's always had one but now he's got two.❞

National Team Managers
Terry Venables...

"There are two ways of getting the ball. One is from your own team-mates, and that's the only way."

"If history repeats itself I should think we should expect the same thing again."

"The lad's nose was all over the place and he was angry." – On Hamilton Ricard's broken nose.

"If you can't outplay the opposition, you must out number them."

"If you can't stand the heat in the dressing-room, get out of the kitchen."

"It's understandable and I understand that."

BELOW "Join me and I'll have you in the England squad in six weeks." – on Gazza signing for Spurs

"The spirit he has shown has been second to none."

"The Uruguayans are losing no time in making a meal around the referee."

"It may have been going wide, but nevertheless it was a great shot on target."

"Certain people are for me and certain people are pro me."

"They didn't change positions, they just moved the players around."

"I felt a lump in my mouth as the ball went in."

"It was never part of our plans not to play well, it just happened that way."

National Team Managers
Glenn Hoddle...

BELOW "Robert Lee was able to do some running on his groin for the first time."

"75 per cent of what happens to Paul Gascoigne in his life is fiction."

"With hindsight, it's easy to look at it with hindsight."

"The minute's silence was immaculate. I have never heard a minute's silence like that."

"Football's all about 90 minutes."

"I think in international football you have to be able to handle the ball."

"Look at Jesus. He was an ordinary, run-of-the-mill sort of guy who had a genuine gift, just as Eileen has." — Hoddle defends the appointment of faith healer Eileen Drewery to the England backroom staff.

"We didn't have the run of the mill."

"Okay, so we lost, but good things can come from it – negative and positive."

"But he was a player that hasn't had to use his legs, even when he was 19, because his first two yards were in his head."

"I have a number of alternatives, and each one gives me something different."

"His tackle was definitely pre-ordained."

"I think I must have run over six black cats since I've been at Wolves."

"When a player gets to 30, so does his body."

"International football is one clog further up the football ladder."

National Team Managers
Best of the Rest...

"If I walked on water, my accusers would say it is because I can't swim."
– Berti Vogts, coach to the German team.

"Hagi is a brilliant player, but we're not going to get psychedelic over him." – Andy Roxburgh

"In comparison, there's no comparison." – Ron Greenwood

"You don't have to have been a horse to be a jockey." – Arrigo Sacchi, Italy coach, defending a meagre playing record.

"One defeat in 60? Oh Jesus!" – England manager Sven-Goran Eriksson on finding out that his team's opponents, Germany, have only lost once in 60 World Cup qualifying games.

"I sometimes wished I'd been shot ... though it never came to that ... nor should it." – Graham Taylor on his time as England manager.

"Playing with wingers is more effective against European sides like Brazil than English sides like Wales." – Ron Greenwood

"I certainly wouldn't put money on myself. Working as a national manager is out of the question." – Sven-Goran Eriksson, six days before accepting the England job.

"Love is good for footballers, as long as it is not at half-time." – Richard Moller Nielsen, Denmark coach.

"It was a game we should have won. We lost it because we thought we were going to win it. But then again, I thought that there was no way we were going to get a result there." – Jack Charlton

"There is great harmonium in the dressing room." – Sir Alf Ramsey

BELOW Sven-Goran Eriksson.

ABOVE "There will have to be a bubonic plague for me to pick Di Canio." – Italy coach Giovanni Trapattoni.

Life in the Lower Leagues...

"Football is a game of skill, we kicked them a bit and they kicked us a bit." – Graham Roberts

BELOW Ian Holloway.

"No disrespect to the lads here but there are seven or eight of them that we are trying to get off the wage bill. We cannot even give them away at the moment!" – Huddersfield Town chairman Ian Ayre on a surplus of players.

"I would buy some bad players, get the sack and then retire to Cornwall." – Sheffield United boss Neil Warnock, when asked what he would do if he was manager of city rivals Sheffield Wednesday.

"Darlington will become the most successful club in England." – George Reynolds

"Chester made it hard for us by having two players sent off." – John Docherty

"I'm the happiest man alive. It feels like I've won the Lottery. And I share a dream with the board – competing in the Premiership. The passion and commitment at this club from top to bottom is just fantastic. We're not instant coffee here, this is long term." – QPR boss Ian Holloway on signing his new three-year contract.

"We started poorly, we finished poorly and we were poor in the middle. Even when we were 1–0 up after five minutes I knew it was a disaster waiting to happen." – Bournemouth player/coach Peter Grant.

"I've told the players we need to win so that I can have the cash to buy some new ones." – Chris Turner, Peterborough manager, before a League Cup quarter-final in 1992.

ABOVE "Alessandro del Piero reminds me of Robert Rosario when I had him at Coventry." – Bobby Gould

"I did enough algebra at university and I'm sick of it. We have to focus on our own business, starting with Saturday's home game with Birmingham.**"** – Qualified aeronautical engineer Iain Dowie hasn't worked out his relegation equations.

BELOW Steve Coppell.

"Plenty of goals in Divisions 3 and 4 today. Darlington nil, Hereford nil.**"** – Radio 2

"I'm a man of few words, but most of the ones I said to the players began with F.**"** – Reading manager Steve Coppell, following his side's 4–1 defeat at Wolves.

"I've been dying to leave Gary out. He's got a cold, he's got a knock on his foot, his face is full of cold sores – other than that he's a good-looking lad. I wanted to give him a rest as well.**"** – Burnley boss Steve Cotterill on Gary Cahill.

"I thought we were poor from start to finish and overall I don't think they were much better.**"** – Boston boss Steve Evans provides a cheery summary of his side's match with Northampton.

"Managing is a seven-day-a-week, almost 24-hour-a-day job. There's no rest and no escape, but I'm hooked on it.**"** – Barry Fry

"He led with his head, he didn't head-butt.**"** – West Ham boss Alan Pardew on Tomas Repka's head-butt which led to a red card against Preston.

"Dave has this incredible knack of pulling a couple of chickens out of the hat each season.**"** – Millwall manager Mark McGhee attempts to pay homage to Dave Jones of Wolves.

ABOVE "I was sitting with my girlfriend feeling very unfulfilled." – The then Wycombe boss Tony Adams on why he wanted to get back into football.

Best of the Rest...

BELOW Martin O'Neill.

ABOVE "As I've said before and I've said it in the past ..."
– Kenny Dalglish

"It's sod's law. Now I've got time to improve my golf it's the wrong time of year." – Howard Wilkinson, on being sacked by Leeds.

"Our first goal was pure textile." – John Lambie

"What I said to them at half-time would be unprintable on the radio." – Gerry Francis

"That's great, tell him he's Pele and get him back on." – John Lambie, Partick Thistle manager, when told a concussed striker did not know who he was.

"We must have had 99 per cent of the game. It was the other three per cent that cost us the match." – Ruud Gullit

"Players who have more great games than other players are the great players." – Graeme Souness

"If we'd won, it would have meant an historic double-treble. But we weren't even thinking about that." – Walter Smith

"Zinedine Zidane could be a champion sumo wrestler. He can run like a crab or a gazelle." – Howard Wilkinson

"He's a water carrier, a hard worker, a bit of a dog ... a ferret." David Pleat on Didier Deschamps.

"If they hadn't scored, we would've won." – Howard Wilkinson

"Wendy Toms has never been taken from behind by a 14-stone centre-half." – Joe Royle

"Ken Bates is a football cretin." – Martin O'Neill

"What the f**k is art? A picture of a bottle of sour milk lying next to a smelly old jumper? What the f**k is all that about?" – John Gregory commenting on art, what does he know about it?

"Klinsmann has taken to English football like a duck out of water." – Gerry Francis

"Manchester United take more in programme sales than we take on the gate." – Lawrie McMenemy, the then Southampton manager.

"Achilles tendon injuries are a pain in the butt." – David O'Leary

"Give him his head and he'll take it with both hands or feet." – Bobby Gould

"We gained more from the game than they did ... except they got the points." – Brian Little

"We're going to start the game at 0-0 and go out and try to get some goals." – Bryan Robson

"If you buy a man who is half-dead, everybody may be happy off the field, but on the field you'll have major problems." – Arsene Wenger

"A lot of hard work went into this defeat." – Malcolm Allison

"Neil Lennon wasn't sent off for scoring a goal, and that's what annoys me." – Martin O'Neill

"It should be a good match because they're a good football team as well and we're a good football team. It should be a very good match." – Peter Taylor

ABOVE "Of the nine red cards this season we probably deserved half of them." – Arsene Wenger

Best of the Rest...

"Hartson's got more previous than Jack the Ripper." — Harry Redknapp

BELOW Harry Redknapp.

"You must be as strong in March, when the fish are down." — Gianluca Vialli

"My own autobiography, which was written by Ian Ross ..." — Howard Kendall

"The one thing I didn't expect is the way we didn't play." — George Graham

"I like to think it's a case of crossing the 'i's and dotting the 't's." — Dave Bassett

"It's thrown a spanner in the fire." — Bobby Gould

"I promise results, not promises." — John Bond

"I was inbred into the game by my father." — David Pleat

"You weigh up the pros and cons and try to put them into chronological order." — Dave Bassett

"In terms of the Richter scale this was a force-8 gale." — John Lyall

"I can count on the fingers of one hand ten games where we've caused our own downfall." — Joe Kinnear

"Winning all the time is not necessarily good for the team." — John Toshack

ABOVE "Working with people on a field turns me on." — Graeme Souness

"Too many players were trying to score or create a goal." — Gerard Houllier

"I can't sleep, I can't nod off, I can't go out for a beer with the lads like I used to. I think about the job all the time and I'm losing my hair and losing all my mates." – Chris Coleman on the perks of management.

BELOW Peter Reid.

"We have top players and, sorry if I'm arrogant, we have a top manager." – Jose Mourinho

"He is flat out in the dressing room, I just knocked him out. Now I might go round and burn down his house." – Wolves boss Dave Jones on his 'special' relationship with old employee and Southampton scorer Chris Marsden.

"His name was Declan Roche and he was talking back to me – so I got these dead pigeons out of a box and slapped him round the face with one." Partick manager John Lambie on his own 'Bootgate' saga.

"When you are 4–0 up you should never lose 7 1." – Lawrie McMcnemy

"Our major problem is that we don't know how to play football." – Bolton boss Sam Allardyce finally admits it.

"Fergie should send me a decent bottle of red. I'm hoping for a crate but, knowing Fergie as I do, it will probably be a bottle." – Peter Reid after Leeds beat Arsenal to send the Premiership trophy to Old Trafford.

"If I don't have an ambition of managing AC Milan or England then it lies in managing Charlton, for example, which there's an outside chance with the connection I've got. No disrespect to Charlton but is that me fulfilled? No, it's not what I want." – Alan Pardew, who later went on to take the hotseat at the mighty West Ham.

ABOVE "It's a case of putting all our eggs into the next 90 minutes." – Phil Neal

Best of the Rest...

"Luckily they had a stupid on their side, too." – Harry Redknapp warms to Robin van Persie after David Prutton was sent off in Soton's 1–1 draw with Arsenal.

"I can't say yet if I will like him. How can you judge a man until you come face to face? Maybe I'll find out what he's really like over these next few weeks. I know he's very successful but we'll learn a little more about him and his team. So, sure, when we finally meet, it could be quite a moment." – Frank Rijkaard on Jose Mourinho.

"Come on, let's take this lot. They canna' f****n' play!" – Archie Gemmill, heard shouting across the pitch in a U.E.F.A. Cup game against Servette of Switzerland.

"What the f**k did you think you were doing." – What Arsene Wenger supposedly enquired of van Persie as the young Arsenal striker meandered past the animated Arsenal boss on the way to the St Mary's tunnel.

"We just ran out of legs." – David Pleat

"Titus (Bramble) was outstanding but he's got to learn. He's done one thing wrong and that was to come off without there being a break in the play to put his dislocated pinkie back in, the big pussy cat." – Graeme Souness

"You call them mind games? How do they work?" – Frank Rijkaard talking before Jose Mourinho lets rip with his pre-match naughtiness. And after hearing a few examples of Mourinho's taunts, Rijkaard laughed loudly: "Thank you! Thank you! I look forward to this kind of game. What has he said so far?"

"Frank Rijkaard's history as a player cannot be compared with my history. His history is fantastic and my history is zero. My history as a manager cannot be compared with Frank Rijkaard's history. He has zero trophies and I have a lot of them." – Jose Mourinho on Frank Rijkaard.

"We can't win at home, we can't win away. As general manager, I just can't figure out where else to play." – Jock Brown, Celtic General Manager.

BELOW Graham Taylor.

"If you can get through the first round you have a good chance of getting into the next one." – Nigel Worthington

"As long as no one scored, it was always going to be close." – Arsene Wenger

"We did not deserve to lose today – we weren't beaten, we lost." – Howard Wilkinson

"We threw our dice into the ring and turned up trumps." – Bruce Rioch

"We're on the crest of a slump." – Middlesbrough manager Jack Charlton, 1977

"When he was carried off at Leicester someone asked me if he was unconscious, but I didn't have a clue – that's what he's always like." – Southampton manager Gordon Strachan on Claus Lundekvam.

"To be really happy, we must throw our hearts over the bar and hope our bodies will follow." – Graham Taylor

"Coaches are like fish. After a while they begin to smell" – Trapattoni, the Fiorentina coach.

"The days of professional footballers pouring a crate of lager down their necks after every game have long gone." – Harry Redknapp on life as a young footballer.

ABOVE "If I'd have had a gun, I'd have shot him." – John Gregory on Dwight Yorke's transfer to Manchester United.

"WE DID NOT DESERVE TO LOSE TODAY -- WE WEREN'T BEATEN, WE LOST."

LIMES

HEAVEN

Chapter 3

The Beautiful Game!

Whether you support a leading Premiership team or a struggling lower league side, one of the most entertaining ways to spend a Saturday afternoon is to witness the incredible skill of footballers. Most of us, however, would secretly agree that we enjoy their frequent mistakes just as much as their moments of genius.

In this chapter we look at the world of football from the point of view of the footballers themselves. From the on- and off-pitch exploits of legends such as George Best, to the extraordinary life and times of David Beckham, the sheer stupidity of some of our favourite players can make us laugh (or cry!).

The footballer – truly a breed apart. While some of them may be full of athletic grace and footballing prowess, most seem to suffer from a very serious case of 'foot in mouth' disease.

"MY PARENTS HAVE BEEN THERE FOR ME, EVER SINCE I WAS ABOUT SEVEN."

David Beckham...

BELOW Interviewer: "Would it be fair to describe you as a volatile player?" David Beckham: "Well, I can play in the centre, on the right and occasionally on the left side."

"I definitely want Brooklyn to be christened, but I don't know into what religion yet."

"It's going to be difficult for me – I've never had to learn a language and now I do."

"When I was seven I wanted to be a footballer, but when I was 14, I wanted to be a model. Look where it's put me now."

"After I've stopped playing I intend to take a year off, maybe longer. I'll do whatever Victoria's doing, take a holiday and do all the things I can't do as a footballer. What I want to do is travel to the moon. One day I hope to do it if it's possible by the time I retire. The thought of me going terrifies Victoria, but I'd really love to do it."

"Alex Ferguson is the best manager I've ever had at this level. Well, he's the only manager I've actually had at this level. But he's the best manager I've ever had."

"I have come to accept that if I have a new haircut it is front page news. But having a picture of my foot on the front page of a national newspaper is a bit exceptional."

"That was in the past & we're in the future now."

"He walks around the kitchen going 'I'm a gay icon, they love me'. The thing is with David is that he doesn't care. He'll go out in his skirt and his bandana and he doesn't care what people say." – **Victoria Beckham**

"My parents have been there for me, ever since I was about seven."

"I do go to football sometimes but I don't know the offside rule or free kicks – or side kicks – or whatever they're called." – Victoria Beckham

Paul Gascoigne...

"I've had 14 bookings this season – eight of which were my fault, but seven of which were disputable."

"You couldn't make it up".
His interviewer, Brough Scott, on this and the rest of the morning he spent with Gascoigne at the Middlesbrough training ground.

"The plaster cast was due off at the hospital today, but I was bored last night so I decided to cut it off in the kitchen and I spiked myself." – Dr Paul Gascoigne.

"It was a big relief off my shoulder."

"When he was dribbling, he used to go through a minefield with his arm, a bit like you go through a supermarket." – Bobby Robson

BELOW "The most important thing is to get Rangers into the Premiership."

"The doctor at Lazio told me I should try drinking wine, because it would be good for me. When I did, he had one look at me and said: 'You'd better go back on the beer'."

"G8 is right for us now. It sounds a bit like great, or at least it does with my Geordic accent."

"Because of the booking, I will miss the Holland game – if selected."

"Baffled." – On being excluded from I'm a Celebrity Get Me Out of Here.

"Paul's not right for us because it's too closely linked to Gazza." – On his name change to 'G8'!

"I never make predictions, and I never will."

The Foreign Legion...

"It was with a homosexual, I was barely 14 years old. But let's be fair, I wasn't the only one who did it. He was a man in Bauru that all our team visited." — Pele on losing his virginity.

BELOW Pele.

"I would not sign for another club, not even if I was offered 15 million dollars. However, it would be different if they were to instead offer me 15 different women from all around the world. I would tell the club chairman: 'Please let me make these women happy – I will satisfy them like they have never been satisfied before'." — Sasa Curcic

"The doctors have told me that the pain in my Achilles is connected with my teeth. They've advised me to have some teeth taken out but I'm afraid of the dentist and so I kept putting it off." — Vladimir Smicer defies biology.

"I have seen Manchester United so many times on television this season and they were playing really poor football – really rubbish." — Patrick Vieira

"I usually don't have sex. Not on the same day. I say no thanks. I guess that, mentally, I want to keep the feeling in my feet and that's why. I think the feeling sort of disappears out of your feet if you have sex before. I have tried before and my feet felt like concrete when you are supposed to kick the ball." — Freddie Ljungberg

"Francis Jeffers is a disgusting, dirty little t**t." — Sander Westerveld

"Unconsciously, I fell in love with the small round sphere with its amusing and capricious rebounds which sometimes play with me." — Fabien Barthez

"I like the comfort of jeans, and the elegance of a suit. But above all, I love the sensuality and sexuality that emanates from leather. It multiplies one's sensations tenfold." — Emmanuel Petit

ABOVE "Sometimes in football you have to score goals." — Thierry Henry

"If I run, I run with meaning, and only at the right moment. Not like a chicken without a head. My style is to think before I get the ball so that when I get it, I know what I'm going to do with it." – **Patrick Kluivert explains away his apparent indolence.**

"I was settled at Manchester United, I had even just ordered a new kitchen, but they wanted to sell me. If a club wants to sell you, there is nothing you can do. You can be sold like cattle." – Jaap Stam

"Ferguson didn't give me enough time to be a success. He lacked patience and it seemed I would always be the scapegoat. I got tired of being a substitute for Ruud Van Nistelrooy. The manager only had eyes for the Dutchman. And Roy Keane didn't like me from the moment I arrived." – Uruguayan striker Diego Forlan, who has scored 13 goals since joining Villarreal and is La Liga's second highest scorer after Barcelona's Samuel Eto'o.

"We made this happen and my wife forced me. Depor forced me to go by deliberately screwing up a move to Fiorentina. Now I am in Birmingham instead of Florence. Only a madman would want to come here." – New Birmingham signing Walter Pandiani.

"The Premier League is a great competition. It is an honour for me to play in England and for Birmingham." – The same Walter Pandiani a day later.

"I don't really like the north. It's always raining, it's really cold and I don't like all those little houses." – Freddie Kanoute

"I'd like to be a dog. Dogs are nice. They can sleep any time, they wag their tails and on top of that they can get stroked all the time." – Emmanuel Petit

ABOVE "I am a Nigerian and I will remain a Nigerian until the day I die." – Kanu

George Best...

❝...I'd give all the Champagne I've ever drunk to be playing alongside him in a big European match at Old Trafford...❞
– About Eric Cantona

❝It's a pleasure to be standing up here. Indeed, it's a pleasure to be standing up.❞
– Accepting his Footballer of the Century Award.

❝I've stopped drinking, but only while I'm asleep.❞

❝...I once said Gazza's IQ was less than his shirt number and he asked me... 'What's an IQ?'❞

❝I don't think he's a great player. He can't kick with his left foot, he doesn't score many goals, he can't head a ball and he can't tackle. Apart from that he's all right.❞ – George Best pays tribute to David Beckham.

BELOW "If George had been born ugly, he probably would have played till he was 40... just look at Peter Beardsley." – Paddy Crerand pays tribute to George Best.

❝That's what children do – throw food. That's not fighting. We were real men. We'd have chinned them.❞

❝I used to go missing a lot – Miss Canada, Miss United Kingdom, Miss Germany.❞

A porter enters a hotel room with a bottle of champagne to find George Best in bed with Miss World. There's a pile of five pound notes on the floor and the porter asks, ❝George, where did it all go wrong?❞

❝George is in good spirits.❞ – George Best's spokesman Philip Hughes gives an unfortunately worded progress report on Best's recovery from liver problems.

❝It's typical of me to be finishing a long and distinguished drinking career just as the Government are planning to open pubs 24 hours a day.❞

"I SPENT A LOT OF MONEY ON BOOZE, BIRDS AND FAST CARS. THE REST I JUST SQUANDERED."

National Team Captains...

BELOW Alan Shearer.

ABOVE "If somebody in the crowd spits at you, you've got to swallow it." – Gary Lineker

❝The beauty of Cup football is that Jack always has a chance of beating Goliath.❞
– Terry Butcher

❝No money in the world can buy a white England shirt.❞ – Alan Shearer

❝I've never wanted to leave. I'm here for the rest of my life, and hopefully after that as well.❞ – Alan Shearer

❝It wasn't going to be our day on the night.❞
– Bryan Robson

❝I have always said that the best feeling in the world is scoring a goal. Don't tell my missus that, but it is. When that ball hits the back of the net, it is fantastic.❞ – Alan Shearer

❝One accusation you can't throw at me is that I've always done my best.❞
– Alan Shearer

❝I was really surprised when the FA knocked on my doorbell.❞
– Michael Owen

❝If you never concede a goal, you're going to win more games than you lose.❞
– Bobby Moore

❝I'm not looking to retire. I hope to keep going as long as my legs will take me.❞
– David Beckham

❝There's no way the future's over for Martin Keown, Tony Adams or David Seaman.❞ – Alan Shearer commenting on ageing England players.

❝You've got to believe that you're going to win, and I believe we'll win the World Cup until the final whistle blows and we're knocked out.❞
– Peter Shilton

Best of the Rest...

❝The only thing I have in common with George Best is that we come from the same place, play for the same club and were discovered by the same man.❞ – Norman Whiteside

❝The only way we will be going to Europe is if the club splash out and take us all to Euro Disney.❞ – Dean Holdsworth

❝I'm five short (of the Arsenal goalscoring record) – not that I'm counting.❞ – Ian Wright

❝I'd like to play for an Italian club, like Barcelona.❞ – Mark Draper

❝I was watching the Blackburn game on television on Sunday when it flashed on the screen that George Ndah had scored in the first minute at Birmingham. My first reaction was to ring him up. Then I remembered he was out there playing.❞ – Ade Akinbiyi

❝If you don't believe you can win, there is no point in getting out of bed at the end of the day.❞ – Neville Southall

❝I faxed a transfer request to the club at the beginning of the week, but let me state that I don't want to leave Leicester.❞ – Stan Collymore

❝I would not be bothered if we lost every game as long as we won the League.❞ – Mark Viduka

❝I couldn't settle in Italy – it was like living in a foreign country.❞ – Ian Rush

❝Leeds is a great club and it's been my home for years, even though I live in Middlesbrough.❞ – Jonathan Woodgate

❝He was just about to pull the trigger on his left foot.❞ – Terry Butcher

BELOW Ian Rush.

ABOVE "We lost because we didn't win." – Ronaldo

Best of the Rest...

ABOVE "Winning doesn't really matter as long as you win."
— Vinnie Jones

❝People say footballer's have terrible taste in music, but I would dispute that. In the car at the moment I've got The Corrs, Cher, Phil Collins, Shania Twain and Rod Stewart.❞ — **Andy Gray**

❝I'm an emotional person and I enjoy crying. You know the film Beaches with Bette Midler and Barbara Hershey? Sometimes, when I want a good cry I put it on.❞ — Sensitive Ian Wright.

❝Away from home our fans are fantastic, I'd call them the hardcore fans. But at home they have a few drinks and probably the prawn sandwiches, and they don't realise what's going on out on the pitch.❞ — Roy Keane

❝Dennis Wise, Vinnie Jones and John Fashanu must be turning in their graves.❞ — **Carlton Palmer**

❝I'm as happy as I can be — but I have been happier.❞ — Ugo Ehiogu

❝The opening ceremony was good, although I missed it.❞ — Graeme Le Saux

❝I hate to admit this but I don't even know how to make a cup of tea or coffee. I can boil a kettle for a pot noodle and I've been known to warm up some food in the microwave.❞ — Michael Owen

❝Right ankle, right hand and right side of my forehead — I'm sick. I tried to get on to the team bus after the game with crutches but I couldn't because of my right hand! I was a bit of a mess, really, but there you go.❞ — Alan Shearer in a RIGHT mess.

❝When you're walking onto a bus and trying to get there before the person in front of you, that's a different level of competition to playing in front of 80,000 people.❞ — Graeme Le Saux

Reporter to Newcastle's Shola Ameobi: **Do you have a nickname?** Ameobi: **No, not really.** **Reporter:** **So what does Bobby Robson call you?** Ameobi: **Carl Cort.**

I was surprised, but I always say nothing surprises me in football. – Les Ferdinand

He was on the pitch going on about how much money he was on. He is a top player but he just never shuts up. He was going on at everyone in our team. I think that's why he is not liked. Let the football do the talking with his ability and he could shut anyone up. But Bellamy? Dearie me, he was worse than my kids.
– Clyde midfielder Darren Sheridan.

He (the Doctor) tried everything. I had goose liver, calf's liver and juices from a turkey's head injected into me. – Dominic Matteo, on how his doctor went mad in the fresh meat section.

I gave away the foul that Leeds scored one goal from, then put the ball into my own net from their free-kick. I don't want to say I lost us the championship, but... – Ashley Cole on his man-of-the-match performance.

I would have him (Smith) there for England ahead of Emile Heskey because, with respect, I could score more goals than him at age 56! – 1970s England striker Allan Clarke.

I always used to put my right boot on first, and then obviously my right sock. – Barry Venison

When we go out in the evening I like to go for it. I love the traditional English gentleman look with cuff-links, highly-polished shoes and even a money clip. – David Seaman

I'm a London boy but I am also a great lover of football – although Real Madrid and Barcelona are not quite looking at me at the moment! – Jody Morris

ABOVE Interviewer: "Which is your favourite commentary team, BBC or ITV?" Graeme le Saux: Sky.

Best of the Rest...

BELOW Steve McMahon.

ABOVE "I've got a good record there – played one, won one – hopefully it will be the same after Saturday..."
– Steven Gerrard

"I know I can't go on forever – how can I forget it when my so-called team-mates keep asking me which king was on the throne when I started and what football was like in the Dark Ages!" – Les Ferdinand

"I am not Pele or Maradona." –Robbie Savage

"...When I arrived at Liverpool, I was at my peak and an England international. Now I'm a Pontins League player..." – Nigel Clough

"I could have signed for Newcastle when I was 17, but I decided I would be better off at Carlisle. I'd had a drink that night." – Peter Beardsley

"I'd kick my own brother if necessary... it's what being a professional footballer is all about." – Steve McMahon

"As I came to shoot, a defender stopped and half-turned his back on me. If he'd taken another step it would have been very difficult for me to get the ball past him. They say the book of Italian heroes is very thin... and he wasn't into expanding it any..." – Tommy Gemmell

"We all speak English, but Carragher talks very strange English." – Stephane Henchoz

"He (Souness) has just gone behind my back in front of my face." – Craig Bellamy

"It's a St Valentine's Day box of chocolates, one that I am going to enjoy and I hope that when I unwrap it, it has got a soft centre." – Iain Dowie

"If you're 0–0 down, there's no-one better to get you back on terms than Ian Wright." – Robbie Earle

"I can't even remember when the '70s was." –Robbie Keane

"We took turns from the spot. If you missed one you had to take off your shirt. If you missed another, off came your shorts and then your socks, and so on. In the end you would end up in goal stark naked with everyone booting footballs at you. It was a great laugh!" – **John Terry**

"If I feel like I want to go another year then I'll see what turns up. My missus thinks I'm mad but she's happy with anything that keeps me from getting under her feet!" – Paul Ince

"I worked hard all my life for this. Those who say I don't deserve anything, that it all came easy, can kiss my arse." – Diego Maradona, shortly before retirement.

"The lino said I was three yards off my line. I don't go that far on holiday." – Bristol Rovers keeper, Kevin Miller.

"If I go on holiday at the end of the season and come back with a big, fat belly and a bald head, then I will pack it in." – Dennis Wise

"I don't think I have played as well as I can for Arsenal, but hopefully in this tournament I can do that." – Ashley Cole

"Ashley's a great player, I'm not denying that. But I think if you speak to Ashley, he's Arsenal through and through. It is the same with me, I don't want to ever leave Chelsea." – **John Terry**

"We have a game every three days. How can I be a good husband if I don't make love before each one?" – Frank Leboeuf

"When I was seven I started BMX racing. I could do tricks, and when I was eight I was British champion – but the BMX trophy is the only thing I've ever won!" – Alan Smith

ABOVE "Before games, the smell of burgers wafts down from the stands." – Gary Neville

Best of the Rest...

ABOVE "You must be as strong in March, when the fish are down."
– Gianluca Vialli

Rob Shepherd: "Was there a game last season in which Blackburn's season turned around?" Kevin Gallagher: "Yes, when we beat Liverpool 2–0." Shepherd: "And was there something in that game which made you think that the season was about to turn round for you?" Gallagher: "Well, we scored three goals."

"The boss keeps those things up his sleeve, close to his chest." – Craig Burley

"I couldn't really jet off to the States on a whim and a prayer." – David Platt

"I was disappointed to leave Spurs, but quite pleased that I did." – Steve Perryman

"I spent four indifferent years at Goodison, but they were great years." – Martin Hodge

"There are some great defenders here, I just don't know their names." – David Ginola

"Our consistency's been all over the place." – Andy Hinchcliffe

"My legs sort of disappeared from nowhere." – Chris Waddle

"If you don't concede any goals you'll win more games than you lose." – Wayne Bridge

"We had a belief that we believed in." – Jan Molby

"The important thing is he shook hands with us over the phone." – Alan Ball

"Do you remember when we played in Spain in the Anglo-Italian?" – Shaun Newton

"To be second with one game to go – you can't ask for more." – Stuart McCall

"I dreamt of playing for a club like Manchester United, and now here I am at Liverpool." – Sander Westerveld

"Becks hasn't changed since I've known him – he's always been a flash Cockney git." – Ryan Giggs.

BELOW Ryan Giggs.

"Every striker misses chances, although I can't think of too many I've missed myself." – Ally McCoist

"We were always going to call him Rio although, given what's happened perhaps the timing wasn't right. However, it was quite fitting because he was one week late." – Henning Berg on naming his newborn son after Rio Ferdinand.

"I used to drive home from Manchester United training along the M56 and there was a left turn for Wilmslow, where I lived, and a right turn for Hale, where Norman Whiteside, Paul McGrath and Bryan Robson lived. I used to say that it was left for under three pints a night and right for more than ten." – Gordon Strachan

"She (Eileen Drewery) gives the players a shoulder to talk to." – Neil Webb

"I've lost count of the times I've played in that fixture. Each one was a memorable occasion." – Trevor Steven

"You usually like to play promoted sides around Christmas. They have got two lungs at the moment. It was hard work." – Paul Merson

"Manchester was a nightmare. I found Ferguson to be bogus as few people are. He kept saying to me 'Next time you will play, don't worry, do you understand?'. Certainly I understood, I understood he wanted me out." – Massimo Taibi.

ABOVE "I wouldn't describe diving as cheating." – David Ginola

Best of the Rest...

> **There's only one club in Europe that you can leave Manchester United for – Real Madrid or Barcelona.**
> – John Aldridge

BELOW John Aldridge.

> **I am not Jesus, I cannot change people's heads, but if you have problems because you are human, it can help to see someone like Paolo Di Canio has done the same.**
> – Paolo Di Canio

> **I always find the people who do criticise are middle-aged, pot-bellied, really scruffy hacks.**
> – Stan Collymore

> **Maybe the mistakes have looked worse because they led to goals.** – Ian Walker

> **I may have handed in a transfer request, but there is no way that I want to leave this club.** – David Eyres

> **You can't do better than a goal on your first start.** – Bobby Zamora

> **We defended like Trojans.**
> – Mike Stowell

> **One night there was me, Robbie Fowler and Robbie's painter/decorator mate and they're playing pool for 20 euros, helping themselves behind the bar, bodies scattered everywhere.** – Steve McManaman

> **Alex Ferguson loves the game and will die on the United bench, I am sure of that.** – Eric Cantona

> **The left foot has helped – it's always been there, but I haven't always had the chance to use it.** – Stig inge Bjornebeye

ABOVE "One fan said 'you old git!' – he's got a point you know."
– Nigel Martyn

I'LL BE GAZZA

OFF THE RAILS

WHAT DO YOU KNOW ABOUT FOOTBALL?

Chapter 4

What on earth do you know about Football?

That is the question asked by many fans about people who express an opinion about Football. Whether it is the necessary, but often annoying intervention of referees. Or the predictable jump on the bandwagon of certain famous or celebrity fans.

In this chapter we take a look at some of the more infamous and diverse individuals in football, and we learn what they think and feel about our wonderful national sport.

The majority of fans tend to despise the Boardroom personalities.
These infamous characters have brought us some of the greatest quotes, whilst their view of the game seems totally at odds with the fans and often seems that we've all been to different games!

From the lower leagues to the upper echelons of the Premiership, we uncover some of the game's hidden depths.

"IT TAKES ONE TO KNOW ONE. I'M SURPRISED MARTIN O'NEILL ACTUALLY KNOWS A WORD AS BIG AS CRETIN."

Famous Fans...

ABOVE "Some people get into rock 'n' roll so they can get a great girlfriend – I actually got into it so I could meet Alan Hansen." – Elvis Costello

"I would dream of running down the left wing and putting the ball in the net at Port Vale FC. And I still have that dream now." – Robbie Williams

"I think I could be the amazing guy who, at 38, is still in the game. A local hero, very sexy, very strong, an amazing dribbler of the ball." – Kenneth Brannagh

"Do I support a London football team? I do. I support Manchester United." – Caprice

"I wouldn't date any more footballers – they're not the brightest of people." – Donna Air

"I missed the team, footballers, and the people in Watford, I missed the camaraderie that I had at the club. You know, you don't spend 15 years of your life at a club... and it wasn't just the football that I loved. It was the community spirit, the spirit after the game whether you won or lost. It was very, very good for me. And now I am delighted to be back." – Elton John

"I like to describe myself as an attacking wing-back, capable of unlocking defences with surging runs or a well-placed pass. My team-mates just call me 'donkey'." – Hugh Grant

"I find Andy Cole's perpetual scowl depressing and his chippiness offensive." – David Mellor

"Like socialism, it's about a collective, and it's about teamwork. But above all, it's f*****g war." – Dennis Skinner MP.

"I'll be rooting for England to do well – so do the job, boys!" – Billie Piper

"One is not amused at that." – Reported comments of Queen Elizabeth on hearing that Sol Campbell's goal against Argentina has been disallowed.

BELOW "He's the most beautiful person I've ever met." – Emily Symons talking about her then fiancé Matt Le Tissier.

"I'm glad that European players can go into the Hall of Fame, because it would be unfair to miss them out just because they don't come from England.**"** – Jo Guest

"I came home unexpectedly one weekend and it looked like I'd been burgled, it was that messy. Furniture tipped up and melon pips everywhere. They all stuck inside the vacuum cleaner. It turned out that he and another player had a couple of drinks one night and ended up playing catch with this overripe melon until one of them dropped it and it burst all over the lounge. The stupid bugger tried to hoover it up with my Dyson.**"** – Sky's Helen Chamberlain recalls renting a room to former Torquay player Mark Ford.

Gary Newbon: "Y'know mate, looking at the remaining games I think you're just going to miss out.**" Guest Jim Davidson: "**Yeah – if we want to get into Europe we're going to have to write a song...**" Newbon: "**Great! Let's hear it then!**" Davidson: "**No ... it's a joke. We'd have to write a song for the Eurovision Song Contest, Gary.**" Newbon: "**Right, and Alan Curbishley's not a very good singer anyway, is he?**" Davidson: "**Er...**" Newbon: "**Anyway, Charlton have got quite a lot of celebrity fans, haven't they, and I know another one who never misses a match is another great pal of mine, the actor Keith Howman from Brush Strokes.**" Davidson: "**His names Karl Howman, Gary.**" Newbon: "**Right, and a massive apology to my great friend Karl Howman from Brush Strokes...**"

"He's a great striker.**"** – Manchester United fan Zoe Ball on David Beckham

"I like watching matches, but I'm not certain about the scoring system. **"** – T4 (Channel 4) presenter June Sarpong.

Famous Fans... Which team do they support? Allegedly

BELOW Peter Kay.

ABOVE Hugh Grant.

Arsenal	–	Jeremy Beadle, Dido, Nigel Benn Matt Lucas (from Little Britain)
Aston Villa	–	Nigel Kennedy, Ozzy Osbourne
Birmingham City	–	Jasper Carrot
Bolton Wanderers	–	Peter Kay, Vernon Kay
Blackburn Rovers	–	Carl Fogarty, Jack Straw
Bristol Rovers	–	Jeffrey Archer, Vanessa Gardner
Bristol City	–	The Wurzels, Tony Robinson, Tim Exell
Chelsea	–	David Baddiel, Michael Caine, Suggs, David Mellor, John Major, Jules Gammond
Everton	–	Paul McCartney, Freddie Starr, John Parrott
Fulham	–	Hugh Grant
Leeds	–	Chris Moyles, Jeremy Paxman
Liverpool	–	Cilla Black, Chris De Burgh, Stan Boardman
Manchester City	–	Liam & Noel Gallagher, Bernard Manning
Manchester United	–	Eamonn Holmes, Ulrika Jonsson, Russell Watson

BELOW Ant & Dec.

Middlesbrough	–	Roy 'Chubby' Brown, Chris Rea
Millwall	–	Des O'Connor, Max Bygraves, Tommy Steele
Newcastle United	–	Ant & Dec, Tony Blair, Jimmy Nail
Notts County	–	Robin Hood and Maid Marion
Nottingham Forest	–	The Merry Men
Portsmouth	–	Tommy Boyd, Fred Dineage
Sheffield Wednesday	–	David Blunkett
Southampton	–	Craig David, David Gower
Southend United	–	Alison Moyet
Sunderland	–	Steve Cram, Kate Adie
Swindon Town	–	Willie Carson, John Francome, Kevin Gardner
Tottenham Hotspur	–	Phil Collins, Patsy Kensit, Emma Bunton, Status Quo, Salman Rushdie
Watford	–	Elton John
West Bromwich Albion	–	Eric Clapton, Frank Skinner
West Ham United		John Cleese, Graham Gooch, Frank Bruno

ABOVE Elton John.

The Chairmen, Board and Directors...

"We'll be signing Elvis Presley next." — Peter Ridsdale

"The facts are that we could be in Europe by 5pm on Sunday while Villa have got no chance." — Birmingham owner David Sullivan.

"O'Leary has done a superb job this season and I'm delighted with him. But whatever he may say, we can challenge the top five next season. The sky is the limit. That's the minimum requirement: the top four." — Doug Ellis

"We are not going to feed those who, as clubs, are inferior to us. Cardiff City are the Celtic giants, not Glasgow Celtic ... Robert Earnshaw is worth more than your total club put together. Only three British clubs can compare with Cardiff City — Liverpool, Arsenal and Manchester United." — Bluebirds chairman Sam Hammam.

"What is written on the back pages of certain newspapers passes me by like an ill wind which I respect not."
— Rupert Lowe

"I'll quit when I can no longer stand up." — Villa chairman Doug Ellis, said whilst sitting down.

"I don't like agents. Anything that puts them under the spotlight is good for football."
— Millwall chairman Theo Paphitis.

ABOVE "Tell the Kraut to get his ass up front. We don't pay a million for a guy to hang around in defence." — NY Cosmos executive, on Beckenbauer's positioning.

"Real have turned themselves from a football club into a circus act. That's great for us. I've never seen a chimps' tea party like it — what's happening now with Beckham." — Bayern Munich deputy chairman Uli Hoeness talking about Real Madrid's pursuit of David Beckham.

"The way we have stayed up this season is by signing 19 players. We cannot do that again next year. We need to reorganise and to bring in a top coach." — Milan Mandaric

"We were not prepared to be pushed around by a bunch of yobbos from North London." — Southampton chairman Rupert Lowe on Glenn Hoddle's move to Spurs as Manager.

DAD HELPS OUT

TELETUBBIE

The Chairmen, Board and Directors
Ken Bates...

"Our fans were systematically abused all evening without any provocation and yet we were fined. A bit like being put in a Nazi concentration camp and being charged an admission fee."

"I got calls from Italy last summer and one agent offered me Gabriel Batistuta. He told me: 'Batistuta wants to come to Chelsea.' I said 'I'm sure he does, but we've stopped signing pensioners'."

"Everybody wants to speak to me now I've got money." – On selling Chelsea.

"The king is dead. Well he's retired anyway." – After selling Chelsea.

"To Lord Fergie, The Best Thing Since Sliced Bread." – The inscription on the medal Ken Bates tried to give Ferguson after Chelsea's win.

"All those toilet rolls coming on from Besiktas fans was orchestrated. They wanted to get the kick-off delayed so they would know what the other result was before our game finished. I said to Roman Abramovich, 'if you fancy making another billion, go and open another toilet factory in Turkey'."

"Makelele? Who does he play for? I've only ever heard of his brother, Ukelele."

"I parted on good terms with Luca Vialli. As he left the room and I led him to the door, we departed with the usual Italian formalities of a bear hug and a kiss."

"We needed someone with bigger pockets than I have got."

"It takes one to know one. I'm surprised Martin O'Neill actually knows a word as big as cretin."

ABOVE "Take Ruud Gullit. I didn't like his arrogance. In fact, I never liked him. But while he was delivering the goods, there was no problem. When he lost the plot he had to go."

"I'm not reading them bedtime stories any more."

The Chairmen, Board and Directors...

"I've not spoken with Balaban other than when he came back to Aston Villa after the summer. I said, 'you're back' and he said, 'you remember me then?' I said, 'I'll never forget you, the money I paid for you, my son'. I also told him he had put some weight on." – Doug Ellis on his rapport with his players.

"This is a message for possibly the best supporters in the world. We need a 12th man here. Where are you? Where are you? Let's be having you. Come on!" – Delia Smith

"I have never been hoodwinked in my life. I usually pride myself on my ability to see straight through people." – Michael Knighton on nearly selling 25 per cent of Carlisle to a former barman posing as a millionaire.

"I left numbers where I could be contacted, but nobody rang from Leicester." – Peter Ridsdale

"Most of the people that can remember when we were a great club are dead." – Notts County chairman

"West Ham can take it or leave it. Our £15 million bid for Rio Ferdinand already constitutes a world record for a defender and is a measured valuation. There will be no more." – Leeds chairman Peter Ridsdale, less than a week after upping his final offer by £3 million.

"We came off life support on Friday and are now in recuperation." – Gerald Krasner, the new chairman of Leeds.

"The fans might have envisaged a long string of away defeats strung together like a pearl necklace but we have shown that will not be the case." – Manchester City chairman David Bernstein.

"I've got a gut feeling in my stomach." – Alan Sugar

"I didn't want to be known as the man who shot Bambi." – Newcastle chairman Freddy Shepherd speaks about sacking Bobby Robson

ABOVE "I've felt like the fire brigade on Guy Fawkes Night for the past few weeks." – David Dein, the Arsenal vice-chairman, on the saga of whether Patrick Vieira would go to Real Madrid.

The Referees...

"Neil Warnock has been to my dressing room and we have parted as friends, shaken hands and said good luck. In the heat of the moment, some things are said to the media before other things are said in private, but there are no bad feelings between us." – Referee Graham Poll

"I looked long and hard and decided that if I gave a penalty, I would have had to send off Ferguson." – Referee Mike McCurry explains why he didn't give Aberdeen a clear-cut penalty against Rangers.

"I shouldn't really say what I feel, but Poll was their best midfielder on the pitch. You saw him coming off at half-time and at the end. He smiled so much, he obviously enjoyed that performance." – Neil Warnock

"He (John Hartson) had a go at Stuart McCall as he passed him. Then he was trying to goad Wayne Jacobs, calling him a ginger-haired so-and-so." – Bradford official Derek Taylor.

"I don't like your face." – The reason given by French referee Michel Leduntu after brandishing a red card at PSG's Laurent Roberto.

"I think the referee (Poll) should be banned." – Neil Warnock

"The linesman flagged initially because he thought I was an Oldham player. Fair enough, I did have a replica shirt on – but I also have a big furry head." – Kevin Williams, the man inside the costume of Chaddy the Owl, Oldham's mascot, was offside more than once against Peterborough.

"As referees, we have also become hesitant about giving penalties because of the cancer of simulation. Some dives have been so embarrassing, particularly those in midfield, that I just join in the laughter and don't give a booking but the only way we can stop simulation is to give a caution." – Referee Graham Poll.

ABOVE "If the players want to make it hard for me, I am happy to make it twice as hard for them." – Wendy Toms

"England are looking for a scapegoat and they are looking to blame me." – Swiss referee Urs Meier after disallowing England's late Euro 2004 'winner' against Portugal.

"The referee couldn't wait to book me last night. I got fouled in the corner, got up and asked the referee why he didn't give the free-kick and he just got the yellow card out. I was amazed to be singled out. When you think about diving I don't believe the first player who comes to mind is me but for some reason the referees seem to like talking about it. Graham Poll said it and there was another referee doing an after-dinner speech who mentioned it as well." – Gary Neville feels vicitmised by referees.

"Effectively there's nothing in the laws that prevents it happening. They [Chelsea] have been a little more sophisticated and a little different. The Football Association were aware of it, and it's legal. If he were to take a Christmas hamper on to the pitch it may be a different matter." – Referees' chief Keith Hackett explains Chelsea's system of getting tactics across to players on tiny bits of paper.

"A fat little toy with bulging eyes." – Italy's La Repubblica describes Byron Moreno, who refereed in their defeat against Korea.

"Referees can make mistakes and it's just a co-incidence that many of those mistakes are at Old Trafford and go in favour of Manchester United." – Kevin Phillips finds a clever way of avoiding a FA rap.

"We burn referees like that at the stake." – Paolo Maldini on Graham Poll, after the latter referees Italy's defeat to Croatia.

"We can't accept that one of our best referees has been forced to quit because of this. People like Mourinho are the enemy of football." – Volker Roth, chairman of UEFA's Referees' Committee, attacked Jose Mourinho after referee Anders Frisk resigned.

ABOVE "Because you're Australian and you always beat us at everything" – Referee David Elleray explains a booking for Birmingham's Stan Lazaridis.

The Referees...

"They aren't referees, but the thieves of dreams." – Il Messaggero, after one too many decisions go against the Azzuri.

ABOVE "I don't like trousers that are too tight." – Pierluigi Collina on his new modelling career.

"Graeme's (Souness) head is boiling at the minute so we're best keeping him away from the referee. It was a real disappointment because their equaliser involved a blatant hand-ball by Louis Saha as well." – Dean Saunders

"They were caused by the referee who was an absolute clown. I am annoyed because there were so many incidents in the game including when Andy Hessenthaler rugby-tackled Andy Reid in a three-on-two situation and the referee only showed him a yellow card." – Joe Kinnear on referee Phil Crossley after Nottingham Forest's 2–1 defeat at Gillingham.

"We had one penalty in 38 games last season and we'll probably only get one this time around. It shows officials have a problem in that area giving blatant free-kicks in the box, which is a penalty. If that had been out of the box he'd have been blowing his whistle, but when it goes in they keep it by their side." – Sam Allardyce is frustrated by referees.

"There is a very fine line between what is frustration and what is dissent. Dissent is a cautionable offence, not frustration. But if they step over that line, and frustration becomes dissent, then that's a caution, and if the language is wilfull and is directed at them, then that's a dismissal offence." – Philip Don.

"I wouldn't want to be an assistant referee because with off-side calls you need to have a visual defect in order to be able to have both positions in view." – The head of the German football association (DFB) has inadvertently confirmed what many have suspected for years – there is something wrong with the eyesight of assistant referees.

“ENGLAND ARE LOOKING FOR A SCAPEGOAT AND THEY ARE LOOKING TO BLAME ME.”
— URS MEIER AFTER DISALLOWING ENGLAND GOAL, EURO 2004

TERRACE TALK

As a Bristol Rovers fan who is married to a Swindon fan, I have had to put up with a lot of soccer banter over the years! This mainly good-hearted banter is one of the main occupations of the vast majority of football fans.

All of us try to make the first clever quip or amusing joke, before our fellow fans have had a chance to get stuck in.

This can result in some of the funniest humour that you are likely to hear, and is one of the reasons why many fans follow the game.

This, and the occasional interjection of football trivia, is a great opportunity to show how knowledgeable you are about the game.

Here we celebrate the wit and wisdom of the football fan, whichever team they may support. Many of the jokes can easily be adapted to suit the majority of football teams.

"WHY DO THEY CALL WENGER HITLER? BECAUSE HE CAN'T WIN IN EUROPE EITHER."

Fan Stories...

"If I wasn't praying for City, just think where we might be." – Manchester City chaplain Tony Porter in the club's official magazine, **CITY.**

"We're fed up with incompetents running our clubs."
– Steve Powell spokesman for the Football Supporters Federation discussing Chairman.

"I prayed Jeff Eckhardt wouldn't score. That's a terrible name."
– Cardiff fan Graham Hall, who had pledged to change his name to that of the first Bluebirds player to score. Hall told The Sun that since the game ended 0–0 he now intends to go under the name of his favourite player, Kevin Nugent.

"When Rioch came to Millwall we were depressed and miserable. He's done a brilliant job of turning it all around. Now we're miserable and depressed." – Millwall fan Danny Baker on 5 Live.

"We don't need the clubs, the FA and the money men telling us what we should sing about."
– Football fan on the FA appointing a 'Chant Laureate'.

"I know it sounds awful, but it just hit me half-way through my stag night that I'd rather be going to the match with the lads than marrying Nicola."
– A Hereford fan, cancelling his wedding to watch the FA Cup game against Aylesbury.

"I want to believe in Houllier's Liverpool. I want to detect a grand plan. I want to stop shouting vulgarities at TV screens every time I spot Vladimir Smicer. Trouble is, I can't do any of these things. I can't look at Djimi Traore without seeing a new-born pony."
– Vincent Hogan, *The Irish Independent.*

"Football today is like a game of chess. It's all about money." – Newcastle United Fan, Radio 5 Live.

A week before the Cup Final at Wembley a few years ago there was an advertisement in The Times which read:
"Man offers marriage to woman supplying Cup Final ticket for next Saturday. Replies must enclose photograph of ticket."

❝As a Villa fan, I was more shocked by the excellent away performance of my team than the Bowyer/Dyer incident. The fight was nearly as funny as the defender who made out he'd been hit in the stomach when blatantly handling Vassell's goalbound shot. He must be eternally grateful that Bowyer and Dyer started 'fighting'.❞ – **Aston Villa supporter.**

❝If you're having a kid, don't even consider puffy names and sh**te names like what people call their kids these days. Otherwise what we gonna get in 20 years' time? The England team full of players called Keanu, Ronan, Ashley and f*****g Chesney. F**k that! Call your kids Alf, Herbert, Len, Frank, Fred and Wilf. And let's get the puffs out of the game once and for all.❞ — **Anon**

❝...what else can we do when we're so weak? We invest hours each day, months each year, years each lifetime in something over which we have no control; is it any wonder then, that we are reduced to creating ingenious but bizarre liturgies designed to give us the illusion that we are powerful after all, just as every other primitive community has done when faced with a deep and apparently inpenetrable mystery?❞ — **Nick Hornby** football fan and writer of *Fever Pitch* discussing our obsession with Football.

❝Don't go now❞ ❝Why not?❞ ❝You'll miss the best bit.❞ ❝What's that?❞ ❝Booing them off he pitch.❞ – **Reported exchange between two Nottingham Forest fans.**

BELOW Thanks Sky... Football First on Sky was superb when discussing the Bowyer/Dyer fight. They condemned the whole incident well and said what a disgrace it was that it had been seen by millions of people. Then proceeded to show the incident from every conceivable angle about 12 times. Now why can't they do that with streakers, eh?

Fan Stories...

"The football had princes and kings, but only one God, without doubt he is Diego."
— Hernán Amez, founder of the Maradonian Church

"In 1986 me and my pal (who isn't even a Latics fan) decided to go to the Plymouth game on a motorbike. Because of the distance we decided to stay in a B&B. We set off early morning in the fog and cold and got into Plymouth at 11.45am. We parked the bike, booked into a B&B and scurried off to the nearest pub for some light refreshments. Seven pints later a Barlows coach turned up. They had a swift half or two but we declined a lift to the ground so we could get an extra pint. In the end we had to get a taxi at 5 to 3. We watched the match (which we lost) although we were top of the league at the time, then we walked out with the crowd and suddenly realised we were lost. Oh dear, none of us remembered the name of the guest house or where the bike was. We spent about three hours walking round the streets until we eventually found the bike. Not recommended!"
— Oldham Athletic fan.

"I wonder what Shankly would have made of the Internet? He would probably have said something like 'if it does'nae play fitba it's nae use to me'." — Liverpool fan

A Dutch football club has banned one of it's fans for posing for a photograph with the local mayor with his penis hanging out.

"In today's mega-million-pound football world, results and trophies are bought by the highest bidder. In the days of the 'Great Man' they were earned through hard graft and respect! His achievements should be remembered – his records may never be beaten. Sleep well young man."
— Nottingham Forest fan on the death of Brian Clough.

ABOVE Angry Dutch fans clubbed together to buy Dick Advocaat a flight home after his team's early poor performance at Euro 2004.

"Blimey, it barely seems possible that Jose could be involved in any more scandal, not with an impending Champions League tie against Bayern? So he's going to quit, is he? Is he, balls. I don't know what is more pathetic, the continual blustering of Mourinho as he does anything to divert attention away from his team or the willingness of the press to lap up every word."
– Non-Chelsea supporting football fan.

Curate Jeremy Tear seemed to have taken Alex Ferguson's plea for football fans to sit down to heart, when he sat in every seat at Altrincham's Moss Lane ground. Jeremy sat in all of the 1,084 seats at the Robin's ground within 32 minutes, raising money for a local charity.

An Arsenal fan was so confident that his team would win a match against Manchester United that he challenged his United-supporting pal to a bet. However, his confidence proved to be misplaced and he ended up with a Manchester United tattoo on his chest. "I was gutted," he said, understandably. "A bet is a bet – but my missus wasn't very happy."

There's a common bond between football fans that is hard to explain... You can go to a derby and hate your mates for 90 minutes and still end up having a drink with them after the match.

A chip shop owner in Leeds has been forced to change the colour of his forks, because they remind local fans of Manchester United. Mick Bailey, who runs a shop near Leeds' Elland Road ground noticed business was tailing off, but had no idea why. Then he realised many of the customers he still had were choosing to use their hands rather than the red forks provided. Realising the Manchester connection was putting people off, he has now switched to wooden forks. "I kept putting out these boxes of plastic forks and on match days the white and yellow ones would go really quickly but the red ones were always left over," he explained. "Basically they won't touch them because red is associated with Manchester United and they would rather eat with their fingers than pick one up. It's got to the point where I've had to throw all the red forks out and start using wooden chip forks because at least then they're a neutral colour. It's unbelievable."

Triva
for Fans...

1. Ally McCoist was Scotland's only goal scorer in Euro '96.

2. QPR were once known as St Judes.

3. During the 1930–31 season, Manchester United lost the first 12 games.

4. Neville Southall made his League debut with Bury.

5. Bob Paisley took Liverpool to Wembley 12 times.

6. Manchester City goalkeeper Bert Trautmann played the last 15 minutes of the 1956 FA Cup final with a broken neck.

7. The cover of The Beatles' album Sergeant Pepper's Lonely Hearts Club Band features former Liverpool striker Albert Stubbins.

8. Yugoslavia qualified for the European Championship in 1992 but were excluded. Their replacements were Denmark, who went on to win the tournament.

9. David Beckham signed for Real Madrid for a staggering £24.5 million from Manchester United.

10. Zinedine Zidane is currently the most expensive footballer in history; he was signed for a colossal £47.5 million, also by Real 'moneybags' Madrid!

11. The Subbuteo table football game was launched in 1947.

12. With 90,000 seats, the new Wembley will be the largest football stadium in the world with every seat under cover.

BELOW Jermaine Defoe of Spurs.

13. Tottenham Hotspur is the only club from outside the league to have won the FA Cup, in 1901.

14. The first Football League side to install floodlights was third division (South) Swindon Town in 1951.

15. Liverpool were the first side to win the European Cup on a penalty shoot-out and the first to win a European trophy by a Golden Goal.

16. Two teams hold the record for the fastest relegations, both being relegated in successive seasons from Division 1 to Division 4: Bristol City (Seasons 1979/80, 1980/81, 1981/82) and Wolverhampton Wanderers (Seasons 1983/84, 1984/85, 1985/86).

17. The oldest football club in the Football League is Notts County FC, which was founded in 1862.

18. Brazil is the country with the most World Cup wins. They have won four times in 1958, 1962, 1970 and 1994.

19. The most valuable soccer shirt was worn by Geoff Hurst during the 1966 World Cup final between England and Germany. The shirt sold for £91,750 at Christies, London, in September 2000.

20. The most goals scored by a goalkeeper in a single match came from a penalty hat-trick by goalkeeper Jose Luis Chilavert (Paraguay) playing for Velez Sarsfield in the Argentine professional League.

21. The most penalties saved in a single season by a goalkeeper is eight (out of ten) by Paul Cooper of Ipswich Town in 1979–80.

ABOVE Roberto Carlos of Brazil.

Triva for Fans...

22. The holder of the title for the most football matches played by a professional player is Peter Shilton (UK). He has played 1,390 senior appearances, including a record 1,005 League appearances.

23. Holland's Pies, one of the biggest producers of the favourite football half-time snack, is based in Blackburn and exports pastry all around the world.

24. Former Liverpool reserve keeper Michael Stensgaard's Anfield career was brought to an end after he managed to dislocate his shoulder while putting up an ironing board.

25. Manchester United player Gary Neville's father is called Neville Neville!

26. David Beckham has played for three clubs. Most recently he has played for Real Madrid and Manchester United, and as a younger player he was on loan at Preston North End.

27. The highest ground above sea level is West Bromich Albion's The Hawthorns.

28. Gary Lineker played for England 80 times, and scored 48 goals. This record is beaten only by Bobby Charlton.

29. The English League was founded in 1888.

30. Both the Greeks and ancient Romans played a soccer-type game which resembled modern football – although in this early version, teams could consist of up to 27 players!

31. Gary Ablett is the only scouser to win the FA Cup with both Liverpool and Everton.

32. Wayne Rooney collected more yellow cards for Everton in his last season than goals.

33. In 1966 when England beat Germany at Wembley to win the World Cup there were 93,802 spectators.

34. The first all-seater stadium in England was Coventry City's Highfield Road.

35. The first League goal was scored on 8 September 1888, by Jack Gordon, a Preston North End player.

36. Andrei Kanchelskis is the only player to have scored in a Merseyside, Manchester and Glasgow Derby.

37. Games played by the English Premier League, regarded by many as the world's best league, are broadcast weekly to 163 countries, attracting an audience of 550 million.

38. Red and yellow cards were first used by FIFA referees during the 1970 World Cup in Mexico.

39. Wayne Rooney's habit of kicking balls into the crowd cost Everton more than £3,000.

40. Numbers were worn on the back of football shirts for the first time on 25 August 1928.

BELOW Gary Ablett.

ABOVE Andrei Kanchelskis.

Football Jokes...

Two Oxford fans are walking along. One of them picks up a mirror, looks in it, and says "Hey, I know that bloke". The second one picks it up and says "Of course you do, you thick tw*t – it's me!".

A bloke goes into Stanstead Airport and manages to eventually get into the departure lounge where his flight home is being called. All around him there are overturned tables, smashed windows, broken computer terminals, upturned chairs and crowd-control barriers lying on the floor.

"Christ, what's happened here?" he asks one of the ground crew.

"Oh yeah ...", he replies. "Absolutely hopeless... we had the Chelsea players in here this morning filming the new Nike ad."

Oxo were going to bring out a Euro 2004 Commemorative cube painted red, white and blue in honour of the England squad. But it was a laughing stock and crumbled in the box.

Big Ron was caught speeding on his way to the City ground today. "I'll do anything for three points", he said when questioned.

Which part of a football ground is never the same from one day to the next? The changing rooms.

When the manager of a Third Division club started to discuss tactics, some of the team thought he was talking about a new kind of peppermint.

Why did Chelsea go on the stock exchange? To prove that crap can float.

ABOVE How does Stan Collymore change a lightbulb? He holds it in the air, and the world revolves around him.

Did you hear that the British Post Office has just recalled their latest stamps? Well, they had photos of Manchester United players on them – folk couldn't figure out which side to spit on.

CUP FINAL TICKET

VALENTINES DAY

Football Jokes...

What would David Beckham's name be if he was a Spice Girl? 'Waste of Spice'.

The fire brigade phones Arsene Wenger in the early hours of Sunday morning.
"Mr Wenger sir, Highbury is on fire!"
"The cups man! Save the cups!" replies Arsene.
"Uh, the fire hasn't spread to the canteen yet, sir."

Apparently, when Harry Redknapp was West Ham manager he offered to send the squad on an all-expenses-paid holiday to Florida but they declined. They'd prefer to go to Blackpool to see what it's like to ride on an open-top bus.

On the golf course with David Seaman, Becks spends ages lining up a shot. "Come on," says the goalkeeper. "Get a move on." "Sorry mate," says Becks. "It's just that I know Victoria is watching from the clubhouse and I want to make the perfect shot." "Nah," says Seaman. "You'll never hit her from there."

What have Chelsea and a three-pin plug got in common?
They're both useless in Europe.

Why do they call Wenger Hitler? Because he can't win in Europe either.

What do Aston Villa fans use as birth control? Their personalities.

How can you tell when Leeds are losing? It's five past three.

A Chelsea supporter goes to his doctor to find out what's wrong with him. "Your problem is you're fat," says the doctor. "I'd like a second opinion," the man responds. "OK, you're ugly too," replies the doctor.

Why do Wimbledon fans carry lighters with them? Because they lose all their matches!

What's the difference between a Liverpool fan and a coconut? You can get a drink out of a coconut!

If you see a Liverpool fan on a bike, why should you never swerve to hit him... ? It might be your bike...

Sunderland manager Peter Reid walked into the Nationwide Building Society one day whilst a robbery was in progress. One of the robbers hit him over the head and knocked Reidsy out. Whilst coming around, Reid said: "Christ, where the hell am I?" One of the staff told him he was in the Nationwide. Reid replied: "It's May already then!"

A wee fella hands over a £50 note to the turnstyle operator at St James Park. Fella: "Two please." Turnstyle Operator: "Will that be defenders or strikers, sir?"

What do you call a dead Tottenham supporter in a closet? Last year's winner of the hide and seek contest.

What should a team do if the pitch is flooded? Bring on their subs!

What happens when the opposition cross the halfway line at Villa Park? They score.

How many Bristol City supporters does it take to unscrew a lightbulb? Both of them.

What do you call a Leeds fan in a three-bedroom semi? A burglar.

A goalkeeper had suffered a particularly bad season and announced that he was retiring from professional football. In a television interview he was asked his reasons for quitting the game. "Well, basically," he said, "it's a question of illness and fatigue." "Can you be more specific?" asked the interviewer. "Well," said the player, "specifically the fans are sick and tired of me."

How can you tell ET is a Rangers fan? Because he looks like one.

The seven dwarfs are down in the mines and there is a cave-in. Snow White runs to the entrance and yells down to them. In the distance a voice shouts out: "Arsenal are good enough to win the European Cup". Snow White says: "Well at least Dopey's alive!"

ABOVE What's the difference between a box of Sellotape and Phil Neville? One's a glueless kit!

Football Jokes...

The FA had to step in to prevent Hartlepool's latest sponsorship deal. They signed a mega new contract with the pet-food firm Spillers. A FA spokesman said that it would be fraud to have Hartlepool players with 'Winnalot' on their shirts!

A young autograph hunter was really chuffed when he got Emile Hesky's autograph after a match. The following week he accosted Hesky once more for his autograph, and after the next game he tried to get it yet again. "Look here," said Hesky, "this is the third time you've asked for my autograph. What's going on?" "Well," said the young man, "if I can get eight more of yours, I can swap them for one of Michael Owen's."

Gazza: "Wahey boss! ken that jiggisaw puzzle I wiz doing? Yeel never guess – I've finished it and it only took me six months!"
Walter Smith: "Well, what's so good about six months?"
Gazza: "Like it says gaffer – on the box it said 'three to six years'."

Apparantly, Blackburn football club is under investigation by the Inland Revenue for tax evasion. They've been claiming for silver polish for the past 30 years.

Why do Hearts fans plant potatoes round the edge of Tynecastle?
So they have something to lift at the end of the season.

What's the difference between Alex Ferguson and a jet engine? A jet engine eventually stops whining.

What's the difference between OJ Simpson and England?
OJ Simpson had a more credible defence.

ABOVE What is the difference between Bill Clinton and Man Utd striker Diego Forlan? Clinton can score.

Did you hear about the Scotsman who went down to Wembley for an international match between Scotland and England? When he returned home, one of his mates said, "Was it a big gate, Jock?" "It was that," he replied. "One of the biggest I've ever had to climb over."

A father and son were eating breakfast. The father's newspaper had the headline "Van Gogh sold for £8 million". The son asked: "is he worth it, Dad?" The father, surprised at his son's interest in fine art, replied: "I suppose so, son. Why do you ask?" The son said: "Well, Liverpool paid more than that for Stan Collymore, and he was crap."

What's the difference between a Sunderland fan and a trampoline? You take your shoes off to jump on the trampoline.

What's the difference between a smart Burnley fan and the Loch Ness Monster? The Loch Ness monster's been seen.

Bobby Robson goes into the showers after a game and there is a huge turd in the middle of the floor. He goes back into the changing rooms and says: "Hey lads, who's shit on the floor. Up pipes Duncan Ferguson: "Me boss, but I'm great in the air".

What does EIDOS, Manchester Cities sponsor stand for? ELEVEN IDIOTS DREAMING OF SUCCESS!

Name three football clubs that contain swear words? Arsenal, Scunthorpe and F*****g Man Utd.

What do you call a Swindon fan with half a brain? Gifted.

What's the difference between Stan Collymore and God? God doesn't think he's Stan Collymore.

What's the difference between West Ham and an albatross? An albatross has got two decent wings.

"We're starting up an amateur football team. Would you care to join?" "I would, yes, but I'm afraid I don't know the first thing about football." "That's all right. We need a referee as well."

A football player had dislocated his shoulder in a nasty challenge, and was still screaming in agony when they got him to hospital. "For Heaven's sake," said the doctor, "don't be such a baby; you're supposed to be a big, tough defender. There's a woman having a baby next door and she's not making anything like the noise that you are." "That's as may be," wailed the footballer, "but, in her case, nobody's trying to push anything back in."

Football Jokes...

What do you call a Middlesbrough fan in a suit? The accused.

A man walked into the office of a large London firm and said to the manager: "I'm young Murphy's grandfather – he works in your mail room here. I just popped in to ask if you could give him the afternoon off so I could take him to the League final at Wembley." "I'm afraid he's not here," said the manager. "We already gave him the afternoon off to go to your funeral."

An anxious woman goes to her doctor. "Doctor," she asks nervously, "can you get pregnant from anal intercourse?" "Certainly," replies the doctor, "Where do you think Newcastle fans come from?"

What happens to a footballer when his eyesight starts to fail? He becomes a referee.

Worried that his reputation for not being the sharpest pencil in the box is beginning to affect his career, David decides to go back to school for a bit. After the first week, Posh goes to pick him up at the end of the day and gets talking to one of his teachers.
"How's he doing?" she asks.
"Very well," says the teacher.
"He's made straight 'As'."
"That's marvellous!" says Posh. "Absolutely," says the teacher. "His 'Bs' are a bit wonky, but we'll start on those next week."

How did the football pitch end up as a triangle? Somebody took a corner!

Top tip for Manchester United fans: Don't waste money on expensive new kits every season. Simply strap a large inflatable penis to your forehead, and everyone will immediately know which team you support.

What did the Liverpool supporter do after his team beat Real Madrid? Get out of his armchair and turn off the PlayStation!

How many Evertonians does it take to change a lightbulb? As many as you like, but they'll never see the light.

First child: "It says in my history book that Anne Boleyn had three nipples."
Second child: "That's nothing, Alex Ferguson has got eleven arseholes."

How many Manchester City soccer fans does it take to change a lightbulb? None – they're quite happy living in the shadows.

A Sky television reporter comes to the North East and interviews Bryan Robson and Peter Reid. First of all he speaks to Peter Reid. "So Peter, what are your hopes for Sunderland this season?" asks the reporter. Peter replies: "Well if we can pick up a few points here and there, hopefully we can stay in this division." The reporter then interviews Brian. "So Bryan what are your hopes for Boro this season and in the future?" Bryan replies: "Well we'll piss this division and win the championship and maybe win the FA Cup along the way, then we'll be in Europe..." The Sky reporter interrupts: "Bryan, don't you think you're being a bit ambitious?" "Well Peter started it," replies Bryan.

An Ipswich fan was shopping in the local supermarket. He picked up a tin of soup for one, a small pizza and one pint of milk. He went to the checkout to pay the cashier. The girl on the till asked "Are you single?" "Yes, did you guess from the food?" "No," She replied, "you're f*****g ugly."

What is the best thing to come out of Charlton? The M25.

What did the bumble bee striker say? Hive scored!

A man had tickets to the FA Cup final. As he sits down, a man comes down and asks if anyone is sitting in the seat next to him. "No," he says. "The seat is empty." "This is incredible," says the man. "Who in their right mind would have a seat like this for the FA Cup final and not use it?" He says "Well, actually, the seat belongs to me. I was supposed to come with my wife, but she passed away. This is the first FA Cup final we haven't been to together since we got married in 1967." "Oh... I'm sorry to hear that. That's terrible. But couldn't you find someone else – a friend or relative, or even a neighbour to take the seat?" The man shakes his head. "No. They're all at the funeral."

The Manchester United players are in the dressing room, when, just before the game, Roy Keane walks in. "Boss," he says, "there's a problem. I'm not playing unless I get a cortisone injection." "Hey," says Giggs. "If he's having a new car, so am I!"

ABOVE What's the quickest way out of Wembley? Southgate!

Chapter 6

For all football fans, chants are one of the greatest parts of the game. Whether it's listening to or joining in with the singing, or even making up a 'witty' version of your own, many a happy hour is spent by many a football fan singing along with fellow supporters.

Most chants are directly derived from something that is happening on the pitch. It can be as simple as a ginger or strawberry blonde-haired player or a bald referee that can, often quite spontaneously, inspire a chant.

If you visit different football grounds throughout the country, or indeed the world, you will often hear the same chant with words that have been adapted to suit the local environment.

This final chapter takes you through a selection of the best (and worse!) chants that have been, and in some cases still are, sung throughout football grounds everywhere.

Sing your hearts out for the lads!

Chants — The Players...

PAUL SCHOLES

To the tune of *Kumbayah*.
He scores goals Paul Scholes,
He scores goals,
He scores goals Paul Scholes,
He scores goals,
He scores goals Paul Scholes,
He scores goals,
Pa-ul Scholes, he scores goals.

DENIS BERGKAMP

To the tune of *Winter Wonderland*.
Walking along, singing a song,
Walking in a Bergkamp wonderland.

NUMBER FOUR IS A HORSE'S ARSE

Adapted for any team!
Number four, number four, number four is a
horse's arse,
He's the meanest,
He sucks a horse's p***s,
Number four is a horse's arse,
He looks like a horse's arse!
He smells like a horse's arse!
He IS a horse's arse!

SUNG BY MAN UTD FANS TO JERMAINE PENNANT AFTER A DRINK-DRIVING CONVICTION,

to the tune of *Sing When You're Winning*.
You're getting bummed in the shower,
You're getting bummed in the shower,
Bummed in the shower.

JAMIE CARRAGHER

He's scouse,
He's sound,
He'll t**t you with a pound,
It's Carragher, Ca-rra-gher.

CELTIC FANS SERENADE FORMER RANGERS HERO ALLY MCCOIST IN HIS LAST PROFESSIONAL GAME

There's Only One John Parrot.

SUNG TO RIO FERDINAND ON HIS RETURN

P*** in a bottle,
You couldn't p*** in a bottle,
P*** in a bot-tle...

STEVE GERRARD

To the tune of *Que Sera Sera*.
Steve Gerrard, Gerrard,
He scores from 40 yards,
And also he's f**king hard,
Steve Gerrard, Gerrard.

GILLES DE BILDE – CAN HE FIX IT?

Gilles de Bilde (can he fix it?),
Gilles de Bilde (can he f***?).

SMITHY

Sung by Manchester United.
Smith, Smith, Alan Alan Smith,
He came from Leeds but we don't care,
Alan Alan Smith .

SMITH IS A RED

To the tune of *Oh When The Saints*.
Oh Alan Smith,
He is a Red.
Like Ferdinand and Cantona,
He said f**k-off to Leeds United,
Uh Alan Smith, he is a red.

WE'VE GOT WESLEY BROWN

To the tune of *Knees Up Mother Brown* and sung by Manchester United.
We've got Wesley Brown,
We've got John O'Shea,
And once or twice a season,
We've got David May.

ROBBIE SAVAGE

Middlesbrough fans singing to Welshman Robbie Savage.
Gay in the village,
The only gay in the village.

PATRICK VIEIRA

Sung by Arsenal.
Vieira, whoa-oh oh,
Vieira, whoa-oh oh,
He comes from Senegal,
He plays for Arsenal.

SUPER NICK

Super super Nick,
Super super Nick,
Super super Nick,
Super Nick Anelka.

BELOW Robbie Savage.

Chants — The Players...

ONE MICHAEL OWEN

One Michael Owen,
There's only one Michael Owen,
One Michael Owen,
There's only one Michael Owen.

TEDDY SHERINGHAM

Oh Teddy Teddy,
Teddy Teddy Teddy Teddy Sheringham.

PASCAL CYGAN

Sung by Arsenal.
He's bald, He's s**t,
He plays when no-one's fit,
Pascal Cygan, Pascal Cygan.

BELOW Wayne Rooney.

ANDY GORAM

Kilmarnock fans to the Rangers' keeper after he had been diagnosed with mild schizophrenia.
Two Andy Gorams,
There's only two Andy Gorams .

WAYNE ROONEY — GRANNIES

He shags grannies,
He shags grannies,
He shags grannies ... does our Wayne.

Then he pays them, Then he pays them,
Then he pays them ...does our Wayne.

ERIC CANTONA

Sung by Chelsea fans after Cantona had left Leeds.
Où est Cantona?,
Say où est Cantona?

GARY NEVILLE

Neville Neville, you play in defence,
Neville Neville, your play is immense,
Neville Neville, like Jacko you're bad,
Neville Neville is the name of your dad.

FRANK LAMPARD

To the tune of *One Man Went To Mow,
went To Mow A Meadow* and sung by
West Ham fans to Chelsea fans in a recent
F.A. Cup match.
One man couldn't carry,
Couldn't carry Lampard,
One man and his fork lift truck couldn't
carry Lampard,
Two men couldn't carry,
Couldn't carry Lampard,
Two men and their forklift truck couldn't
carry Lampard.

WHEN SHEARER SCORES

Sung by Newcastle United to the tune of
Hey Baby.
Heeeeeeeeeeeeey hey Shearer!
Uhhhh ah!
I wanna knooooooooooooow how you scored
that goal!

Heeeeeeeccccceeeey hey Shearer!
UH ah!
I wanna knooooooooooooow how you scored
that goal!

GUY IPOUA

Sung by Doncaster Rovers to the tune of
Hey Baby.
Guy, Guy Ipoua,
Oooh ... Aaah,
I wanna know,
If you'll score a goal.

WE LOVE YOU FREDDIE

Sung by Arsenal fans to Freddie Lungberg to
the tune of *You're Just Too Good To Be True.*
We love you Freddie, 'cos you're got red hair.
We love you Freddie, 'cos you're everywhere.
We love you Freddie, you're Ars-en-al through
and through. (Repeat)

DIOUF, DIOUF, DIOUF

Sung to the tune of *Agadoo* by Liverpool fans.
El hadji Diouf, Diouf, Diouf,
He has skill and ability,
El hadji Diouf, Diouf, Diouf,
His pace is extraordinary,
Runs from the left, Runs from the right,
He'll leave defenders, On their knees,
El hadji Diouf, Diouf, Diouf,
We all love El hadji.

Chants – The England Team...

ENGLAND CHANT

Inger-land, Inger-land, Inger-land,
Inger-land, Inger-land, Inger-land,
Inger-land, Inger-land, Inger-land,
Inger-land,
INGER-LAND.
(Repeat for most of the match)

THE GREAT ESCAPE

Da-da, da-da da,
Da-da, da-da da,
Da-da, da-da da-da da-darrr,
ENGLAND.
(Repeat for most of the match)

IF IT WASN'T FOR...

If it wasn't for the English you'd be Krauts,
If it wasn't for the English you'd be Krauts,
If it wasn't for the English,
Wasn't for the English,
If it wasn't for the English you'd be Krauts.
(To be sung in France)

TWO WORLD WARS

Two World Wars and one World Cup,
Doo dar, doo dar,
Two World Wars and one World Cup,
Doo dar, doo dar day.
(To be sung whenever Germans are near).

EVERY WHERE WE GO

Every Where we go – Every Where we go,
People wanna know – People wanna know,
Where we come from – Where we come from,
So we tell them – So we tell them,
We're from ENGLAND – We're from ENGLAND,
MIGHTY MIGHTY ENGLAND – MIGHTY MIGHTY
ENGLAND.

SVEN-GORAN ERIKSSON

To the tune of Boney M's *Brown Girl In The Ring*.
Sven-Goran Eriksson,
Na, na, nah, na, nah,
Sven-Goran Eriksson,
Nah, nah, na, na, na, nah, nah,
Sven-Goran Eriksson,
Na, na, nah, na, nah,
He looks like a turnip but he's not,
He's a Swede!

GIVE ME ST GEORGE

To the tune of *Give Me Joy In My Heart.*

Give me St George in my heart,
Keep me English,
Give me St George in my heart I say,
Give me St George in my heart,
Keep Me English,
KEEP ME ENGLISH TILL MY DYING DAY.

HESKEY

If Heskey plays for England so can I,
If Heskey plays for England so can I,
If Heskey plays for England,
If Heskey plays for England,
If Heskey plays for England so can I.

BYE BYE GERMANY

1–0 down,
5–1 up,
Two world wars, and one world cup,
With a knick-nack paddy-wack,
Give a dog a bone,
Germany's f****d off home!

WAYNE ROONEY

I told my mate, the other day,
That I had seen the white Pele,
And he said who, who is he?
And I said he was Wayne Rooney,
Nana na na, nana na na, na na na na , nana na na

OH ENG-ER-LAND

To the tune of *When The Saints Go Marching In.*

Oh Eng-er-land, Oh Eng-er-land,
(repeated by others)
Is full of fun, Is full of fun,
(repeated by others)
Oh Eng-er-land is full of fun,
It's full of t*ts, fanny and English,
Oh Eng-er-land
is full of fun.

BELOW England celebrate after scoring.

Chants —
The Management...

KEVIN KEEGAN

Don't cry for me Kevin Keegan,
The truth is you really blew it,
All through the run-in, though 12 points clear,
You dropped Gillespie, and played Asprilla.

PETER REID – PEELS BANANA WITH HIS FEET

To the tune of *Yellow Submarine* and sung by Newcastle fans.
In the town, called Sunderland,
There lived a man with a monkey's heid,
And they called him Peter Reid,
He peels bananas with his feet,
Peter Reid peels bananas with his feet,
Bananas with his feet,
Bananas with his feet.

ARSENE WENGER

Arsene Wenger's Magic,
He wears a magic hat,
And when he saw the Double,
He said 'I fancy that'.

RAFA BENITEZ

The famous Rafa Benitez went the pub to see the lads and this is what he said, 'Who the f**k are Man United? Who the f**k are Man United? Who the f**k are Man United when the Reds go marching on!' As Benitez stood there, looking at 500 Liverpool fans going mad, a chant from the back started up.

CHEER UP PETER REID

To the tune of *Daydream Believer* and sung by Sunderland FC.
Oh I could fly without wings,
On the back of Reidy's kings,
At three o'clock I'm happy as can be,
'Cos the good times they are here,
And the Premiership is near,
So watch out world as all of Roker sings.

(Chorus)
Cheer up Peter Reid, Oh what can it mean,
To a Sunderland supporter,
To be top of the League,

We once thought of you,
As a Scouser dressed in blue,
Now you're red and white through and through.

A LITTLE TOUCH OF SCOTLAND,
sung by Liverpool FC fans.

A little touch of Scotland came to Liverpool one day,
He looked around and said 'Och man aye, this is where I'll stay',
And from that moment he worked hard to build a team so grand,
And now today we have the greatest team in all the land, Shankly, oh yes Bill Shankly,
Shankly we love you,
For all the things you've done for us while here at Liverpool,
Bill Shankly we thank you.

Nowhere would you find a man who is the same as he,
And all who meet him love him for his humility,
For that and many other things our thanks we give to him,
And do you see we're talking of Bill Shankly.
Aye that's him!
Shankly, oh yes Bill Shankly,
Shankly we love you.
For all the things you've done for us while here at Liverpool. Bill Shankly we thank you.

ALEX FERGUSON
To the tune of *Cheer Up Sleepy Jean.*
Cheer up Alex Ferguson,
Oh what can it be,
To a manc scottish bastard,
And a shit football team.

AH LA LA LA LA BENITEZ
sung by Liverpool FC fans.

Rafa Benitez! Rafa Benitez!
Ah la la la la Benitez!
Ah la la la la Benitez! Xabi Alonso, Garcia and Nunez!

Rafa Benitez! Rafa Benitez!
Ah la la la la Benitez!
Ah la la la la Benitez! Xabi Alonso, Garcia and Nunez!

BELOW Rafa Benitez.

Chants — Scotland...

THE TARTAN ARMY SONG

We'll be coming... We'll be coming...
We'll be coming down yer road,
When ya hear the noise of the tartan army boys,
We'll be coming down yer road!!!

ALL WE ARE SAYING...

To the tune of *All We Are Saying*
(Is Give Peace A Chance)

All we are saying, Is Give us a goooooal,
All we are saying, Is Give us a goooooal,
All we are saying, Is Give us a goooooal.

BELOW Scotland in action, vs Norway.

ENGLAND'S COMING HOME

To the tune of Three Lions.

They're coming home,
They're coming home,
They're coming, England's coming home.

Sung whenever England drop out of any
tournament!

IF I HAD

If I had the wings of a sparrow,
And the arse of a big buffalo,
I'd fly over Wembley tomorrow,
And S***e on the B*******s below.

IF YOU WANT TO GO TO HEAVEN WHEN YOU DIE

If you want to go to heaven when you die,
Wear a Scotland shirt and a Scotland tie,
Wear a Scotland bonet,
With f**k the English on it,
If you want to go to heaven when you die.

WE LOVE YOU SCOTLAND WE DO

We love you Scotland we do,
we love you Scotland we do...
Ohhhhhhhhhhh Scotland we love you.

Chants – Wales...

TOSHACKS CREW

Toshacks Crew Barmy Army!!
Toshacks Crew Barmy Army!!
Toshacks Crew Barmy Army!!

We are red we are white!!
F**k me we are dynamite!!

ALWAYS S**T ON THE ENGLISH SIDE OF THE BRIDGE

To the tune of *Always Look On The Bright Side Of Life.*

Always s**t on the english side of the bridge,
Na na na na na.

WE'LL NEVER DIE

We'll Never Die! We'll Never Die!
We'll Never Die! We'll Never Die!
Keep The Red Flag Flyin' High!
Cause the Welsh Will Never Die!

ARE U ENGLAND?

Are you England, are you England are you England in disguise?
Are you England in disguise?

OH ENGLAND IS FULL OF S**T

To the tune of *When The Saints.*

Oh England, oh England,
Is full of s**t, is full of s**t,
Oh England is full of s**t,
It's full of s**t, s**t and more s**t,
Oh England is full of s**t.

DANCE

Dance, dance, wherever you may be,
We've got a star called Bellamy,
He beats defenders and leaves them on their arse,
Football genius on the park,
He danced round the Danes and got us a win,
He danced round the Argies and fired one in,
He danced round Veron and Cannigia 'cause they're s**te,
And he plays for the boys in red and white.

ALL YOU NEED IS SPEED

All u need is Speed, na na na nna na a,
All you need is Speed, na na na nna na a,
All you need is Speed, Speed,
Speed is all you need.

THREE AND IN

GONE QUIET

Chants — Best of the Rest...

QUE SERA

Que sera, sera
Whatever will be, will be,
We're going to Wem-ber-ley,
Que sera, sera.

THE MEGASTORE IS MAGIC

To the tune of *My Old Man's A Dustman*...
Oh, the megastore is magic,
They sell some magic hats,
And when I saw the duvet,
I said I fancy that,
I even bought the curtains,
And dressing gown in white,
I follow Man United 'cos they sell a lot
of sh*te.

YOU ARE MY SUNSHINE — ASTON VILLA

You are my Villa, my only Villa,
You make me happy, when skies are grey,
I never notice how much I love you,
Until they take my Villa away.

CAN YOU HEAR?

Can you here the Shitty Sing?
No oh,
No oh,
Can you here the Shitty Sing?
No oh,
No oh,
Can you hear the Shitty sing?
'Cos I can't hear a f*****g thing,
Oh oh the Shitty! Ahhhhhhhhhhhhhhhhhh!
(Used for any team who has City in
their name)

LET'S ALL HAVE A DISCO

Let's all have a disco, Lets's all have a disco,
La, la, la, la, Oi, La, la, la, la, Oi.

YOU CAN SHOVE

To the tune of *She'll Be Coming Round The Mountain* and sung to Blackpool fans.
You can shove yer f***ing tower up your arse,
You can shove yer f***ing tower up your arse,
You can shove yer f***ing tower, shove yer
f***ing tower,
Shove yer f***ing tower up yer arse
(Sideways!).

Chants —
Best of the Rest...

ALL FOLLOW SWINDON

Hello, Hello we are the Swindon boys,
Hello, Hello you'll know us by our noise,
And if you are an Oxford fan surrender or you'll die,
WE ALL FOLLOW THE SWINDON.

FLAKEY PASTRY

To the tune of *Coming Round Mountain* sung by Birmingham City fans to Norwich City fans.
Delia can stick her flakey pastry, stick her flakey pastry, stick her flakey pastry up her a**e.

FEED THE SWINDON

To the tune of *Band Aid's Feed The World* and sung by Bristol City fans to Swindon Town fans.
Feeeead the Swindon, let them know its Christmas time, feeeead the Swindon, let them know its Christmas time.

SCORE IN A BROTHEL

Score in a brothel,
You couldn't score in a brothel.

MY GARDEN SHED

My garden shed,
My garden shed,
Is better than this,
It's got a door and a window,
My garden shed is better than this.

COLCHESTER 'TIL I DIE

Colchester 'til i die,
I'm Colchester 'til i die,
I know I am, I sure I am,
I'm Colchester 'til I die.

WE CAN'T READ...

Sung by Cheltenham Town.
Oh, we can't read and we can't write,
But that don't really matter,
'Cos we all come from Cheltenhamshire
and we can drive a tratorrrrrr (tractor).

Ooh Arrr, Ooh Arrr,
Ooh Arrr, Ooh Arrr, Ooh Arrr,
Cheltenhamshire, la la la,
Cheltenhamshire, la la la,
Cheltenhamshire, la la la,
Cheltenhamshire, la la la..

DRINK UP YER ZIDER

Sung by Yeovil Town to the tune of
Drink Up Your Cider by the Wurzels.
Drink up yer Zider,
Drink up yer Zider,
For tonight will merry be, merry be,
We're on our way to Dover,
To shag her in the clover,
There's still more Zider in the jar.
(Repeat)

CAN WE HEAR THE CITY SING?

Sung by Bristol Rovers fans to Bristol City.
Can we hear the city sing? Noooooooooooo!
Noooooooooooo!
Can we hear the city sing,
WE CANT HEAR A F*****g THING!
Ooooooooooa! Oooooooooooow!

ALL GONE QUIET

To the tune of I *Yi Yippie*.
It's all gone quiet over there,
Yes it's all gone quiet over there,
Yes it's all gone quiet,
All gone quiet,
All gone quiet over there.

RUN RUN

To the tune of *Lord Of The Dance*, sung by
Bolton Fans.
Run, run wherever you may be,
We are the BWFC, and we'll tw*t you up,
Whoever you may be,
We'll put you in the infirmary.

SHOW THEM THE WAY TO GO HOME

Sung by Liverpool fans when opposition fans
are going home.
Show them the way to go home,
They're tired and they want to go to bed
(for a w*nk!),
'Cos they're only half a football team,
Compared to the boys in Red.
Oh!

BELOW Liverpool Fans in good voice.

Chants — Best of the Rest...

JUST A LITTLE BOY

Sung by Portsmouth fans to the tune of *Que Sera Sera.*

When I was just a little boy,
I said to my mother,
Shall I be Pompey, shall I be Scum,
Here's what she said to me,

'Wash your mouth out son,
And get your father's gun,
And shoot the Southampton Scum,
And support Pompey!'

BELOW Portsmouth supporters.

ANDY JOHNSON IS MAGIC

Sung by Crystal Palace.

Oh Andy Johnson is magic,
He wears a magic hat,
When he has the match ball,
He say's he's having that,
He scores it with his left foot,
He scores it with his right,
And when we are playing Brighton he
scores all f*****g night.

I WENT A WANDERING (THE CLIFFS OF DOVER)

Sung by Hartlepool fans.

I went a wandering, on the white cliffs o dover,
And if i saw a darlo fan, I'd kick the b*****d over!

WHO ATE ALL THE PIES

Who ate all the pies?
Who ate all the pies?
You fat bastard, you fat bastard,
You ate all the pies.

LET HIM DIE

Let him die, let him die, let him die.

YES!, WE HAVE SOME POSH PLAYERS

To the tune of *Yes!, We Have No Bananas.*

Yes!, we have some Posh players,
We have some Posh players today,
When you're reading the 'Pink-un',
Of old Andy Lincoln, who scored the only goal today –

We've got some fine Posh defenders,
The best that Taylor can send us,
So Yes!, we have some Posh players,
We have some Posh players today.

YOU'RE GONNA GET...

You're gonna get your f****n' heads kicked in.

YOU'RE SO SHIT

You're so shit it's unbelievable.

WORK IN THE SUMMER

As sung to Blackpool fans.

Work in the summer,
You only work in the summer,
Work in the suuuu...mmer,
You only work in the suuu...mmer.

THE PREMIERSHIP IS UPSIDE DOWN

To the tune of *Oh When The Saints* and sung by Bradford fans in 1999/2000.

The Premiership is upside down,
The Premiership is upside down,
We're in Europe with the Wednesday,
And Leeds are going down!

YOU THOUGHT YOU'D SCORED

You thought you'd scored!
You thought you'd scored!
But you were wrong!
But you were wrong!
You thought you'd scored but you were wrong!
You hit the post and we cleared it
You thought you'd scored but you were wrong!

SUNG BY HEREFORD UNITED

The first goal,
The angels did bring,
Was to Hereford United,
And Dixie the king,
Goal, goal, goal, goal,
Born is the king of Edgar Street.

Chants —
Best of the Rest...

YOU ARE

To the tune of *Knick Knack Paddy Whack*.

You are blue, you are white,
Your team is a bag of s***e,
With a knick, knack, paddy whack,
Give a dog a bone,
Take your fans and f**k off home.

ONE SONG

One song,
You've only got one song,
You've only got one song,
You've only got one song.

CHEER UP MARTIN O'NEILL

To the tune of *Cheer Up Sleepy Jean*
Rangers FC

Cheer up Martin O'neill,
Oh what can it be,
To be a f*****g b*****d,
With a s**t football team!

FOUR LEAF CLOVER
Sung by Celtic FC.
(Chorus)

With a four leaf clover on my breast,
And the green and white upon my chest,
It's such a joy for me to see,
For they play football the celtic way.

(Verse)
It's been ten years, long time indeed,
We stood with pride and we took defeat,
Our beloved team, our ancient ground,
Has been rebuilt, a club reborn.

(Chorus)

(Verse)
Mccann he rode the winds of change,
And the things he brought will long remain,
A phoenix rising, a house of steel,
And 60,000 celtic dreams.

(Chorus)

(Verse)
The work is done and the stage is set,
The celtic dream can now be met,
In a sea of dreams, we're here today,
To sit and watch the champions play.

GET YOUR NOSTRILS OFF THE PITCH

Sung to Phil Thompson when at Liverpool.

Get your nostrils off the pitch,
Get your nostrils,
Get your nostrils,
Get your nostrils off the pitch.

WE ARE THE ALDERSHOT

No one likes us,
No one likes us,
We don't care,
We are Aldershot,
Super Aldershot,
We are Aldershot,
From the south.

GOODNIGHT IRENE

Sung to Bristol Rovers

We're loyal supporters, we're faithful
and true,
We always follow, the boys in blue
(and white),
We all made a promise, that we'll never part,
So Goodnight Irene, I'll see you in my
dreams.

WE SHALL NOT BE MOVED

We shall not, We shall not be moved,
We shall not, We shall not be moved,
We've got the team, the score
to win the Football League,
We shall not be moved.

YOU WON THE LEAGUE

Sung to Tottenham Hotspur

You won the league in black and white,
You won the league in black and white,
You won the league in the '60s,
You won the league in
black and white.

BELOW Robbie Keane performs acrobatics, in front of delighted Spurs fans after scoring against West Brom.

Chants — Best of the Rest...

REFEREE

The referee's a w*nk*r, a w*nk*r,
oh the referee's a w*nk*r.

I WAS BORN UNDER AN ORANGE SCARF

To the tune of the *I Was Born Under A Wandering Star,* Sung by Hearts FC.

I was born under an orange scarf,
I was born under an orange scarf,
Do you know where hell is?
Hell is Easter Road,
Heaven is Tynecastle,
Where the Fenians crap their load,
Oh, I was born under an orange scarf.

CHEER UP STAN TERNENT

To the tune of *Daydream Believer.*
Sung by Blackpool FC.

Cheer up Stan Ternent,
Oh what can it be, for those,
Sad Burnley b******s,
And a,
S**t football team.

WE'LL SCORE AGAIN

To the tune of *We'll Meet Again,*
Sung by Exeter City.

We'll score again,
Don't know where, don't know when,
But I know we'll score again some sunny day.

Keep smiling through,
Just like we always do,
'Cos you know we'll score again,
Some sunny day.

Will you please say hello,
To the folks that I know,
And tell them I won't be long,
You'll be happy to know,
While we wait for a goal,
We'll keep singing this song.

We'll score again,
Don't know where, don't know when,
But I know we'll score again some sunny day.

MICKEY QUINN

Sung by Coventry City.

He's fat, he's round,
He scores on every ground,
Mickey Quinn, Mickey Quinn.

WE ALL LIVE IN A RED AND WHITE KOP

Sung by Liverpool FC to the tune of *Yellow Submarine.*

We all live in a red and white Kop,
A red and white Kop,
A red and white Kop,
We all live in a red and white Kop,
A red and white Kop,
A red and white Kop.
(Repeat forever)

THE BLUE FLAG

Sung by Sheffield Wednesday.

Forever and ever, we'll follow our team,
Sheffield Wednesday, we are supreme,
We'll never be mastered by no southern
b******s, We'll keep the Blue Flag flying high.

HE'S ONLY A POOR LITTLE SPURS FAN

Sung by QPR.

He's only a poor little Spurs fan,
He stands at the back of the shelf,
He goes to the bar, to buy a laaaaaa ger,
But only buys one for himself.

NO ONE LIKES US

Sung by Millwall FC.

No one likes us,
No one likes us,
No one likes us,
We don't care,
We are Millwall,
Super Millwall,
We are Millwall From The Den.

THE PRIDE OF ALL YORKSHIRE

Sung by York City.

We are the pride of all Yorkshire, the Cock of
the North,
We hate Leeds United and Scarborough of
course,
We kick in the Toro until they go down,
'Cos the City boys are in town.

I'M TORQUAY UNTIL I DIE

To the tune of *H.A.P.P.Y.* (theme of 1970s
sitcom *Only When I Laugh*).

I'm Torquay 'til I die,
I'm Torquay 'til I die,
I know I am I'm sure I am,
I'm Torquay 'til I die.

Chants —
Best of the Rest...

SOUTHEND PIER

Sung by Southend Utd.

Oh Southend Pier,
Is longer than yours,
Oh Southend Pier is longer than yours,
It's got some shops and a railway,
Oh Southend Pier is longer than yours.

WE ARE NOT SCOUSERS

Sung by Tranmere Rovers.

Do not be mistaken, do not be misled,
We are not Scousers, we're from Birkenhead,
You can keep your cath-e-der-al,
And Pier Head,
We are not Scousers,
We're from Birkenhead.

WE ARE THE WOMBLES

The late, great Wimbledon FC, now MK Dons.

We won't win the League
and we won't win the Cup,
We're not going down and we're not going up,
We're not very good in fact we're bad,
We are the Wombles, we're mad.

THE GREASE CHIP BUTTIE

Sung by Sheffield United.

You fill up my senses,
Like a gallon of Magnet,
Like a packet of Woodbines,
Like a good pinch of snuff,
Like a night out in Sheffield,
Like a greasy chip buttie.

IT'S A GRAND OLD TEAM TO PLAY FOR

Sung by Everton FC.

It's a grand old team to play for,
It's a grand old team to support,
And if you know the history,
It's enough to make your heart go ooooooooooo.

We don't care what the Red s***e say,
What the f**k do we care,
We only know there's going to be a show,
And the Everton boys will be there.

WE SMELL FISH

Sung by Lincoln City to rivals Grimsby Town.

We smell fish, we smell fish.

THE BLUE FLAG
Sung by Chelsea FC.

Forever and ever we'll follow our team,
For we are the Chelsea and we are supreme,
We'll never be mastered by no northern
b*****ds,
And we'll keep the Blue Flag flying high,
Flying high, up in the sky,
We'll keep the Blue Flag flying high,
From Stamford Bridge to Wemb-er-ley,
We'll keep the Blue Flag flying high.

BRIGHTON & HOVE ALBION CHANT

In 1983 we went to Wembley,
To play Man United and make history,
Robbo was through, but he passed it to
Smith,
The stupid Scotch b*****d was pissed and
he missed.

And it's Brighton Hove Albion,
Brighton Hove Albion FC,
We're by far the greatest team,
The world has ever seen.

MARCHING ON TOGETHER
Sung by Leeds United.

Here we go with Leeds United,
We're going to give the boys a hand,
Stand up and sing for Leeds United,
They're the greatest in the land,
Everyday we're all going to say we love you,
Leeds, Leeds, Leeds.
Everywhere we're all going to be there,
We love you,
Leeds, Leeds, Leeds.
Marrrrrrr-ching on, together,
We're gonna see you win,
Cos we're so proud,
We shout it out loud.

BELOW Chelsea celebrations.

Chants —
Best of the Rest...

HENRIK LARSSON.

Sung by Celtic FC to the tune of *Give Me Joy In My Heart.*

Give be joy in my heart, Henrik Larsson,
Give me joy in my hear I pray,
Give me joy in my heart, Henrik Larsson,
Give me Larsson till the end of day,

Henrik Larsson, Henrik Larsson,
Henrik Larsson is the king of kings,
Henrik Larsson, Henrik Larsson,
Henrik Larsson is the king of kings.

BELOW A sea of Celtic fans.

VALLEY FLOYD ROAD

Sung by Charlton FC to the tune of *Mull of Kintyre.*

Valley Floyd Road,
Oh mist rolling in from the Thames,
My desire is always to be here,
Oh Valley Floyd Road.

WHO'S THAT TEAM WE CALL THE RANGERS

Sung by Rangers FC.

Who's that team we all adore,
They're the boys in royal blue and they are,
Scotland's gallant few, and we are out to show
the world what we can do.
So bring on the Hibs, the Hearts, the Celtic,
Bring on Spaniards by the score,
And we will hope that every game, we will
immortalise the name,
Of the boys that wear the famous royal blue.

COME IN A TRAWLER

Sung by Leicester City fans to Grimsby Town fans.

You must have come in a trawler,
You must have come in a trawler,
You must have come in a trawler,
You must have come in a trawler.

DELILAH

Sung by Stoke City.

At the break of day when that man
drove away,
I was waiting,
Oh, oh, oh, oh,
I crossed the street to her house,
And she opened the door,
Oh, oh, oh, oh,
She stood there laughing,
Ha, ha, ha, ha,
I put my dick in her hand she laughed
no more,
Why why why Delilah,
Why why why Delilah,
So before they come to break down the door,
Forgive me Delilah I just couldn't take
any more.

CAN YOU HEAR?

Can you here the Shitty Sing?
No oh, No oh
Can you here the Shitty Sing?
No oh, No oh
Lan you hear the Shitty sing?
'Cos I can't hear a f*****g thing
Oh oh the Shitty! Ahhhhhhhhhhhhhhhhh!

I COMES DOWN FROM SOUTHAMPTON

Sung by Southampton FC.

I can't read and I can't write,
But that don't really matter,
'Cos I comes down from Southampton,
And I can drive a tractor.

I can plough and milk a cow,
And drive a great big mower,
But the thing that I like best,
Is being a strawberry grower,
Oooooo aaarrrrrrr, Oooooo aaarrrrrrr,
Ooooooo to be a Southernerrrrrrrrr.

WE NEVER WIN

Sung by Manchester City.

We never win at home and we never win away,
We lost last week and we're losing today,
We don't give a f**k,'Cos we're all pissed up.

STAND UP IF YOU BOUGHT THE LEAGUE

Sung by Bolton Wanderers fans to Chelsea fan

Stand up if you bought the league,
Stand up if you bought the league,
Stand up if you bought the league.

Chants — Best of the Rest...

BRIDGE FALLING DOWN

Sung by West Ham United to the tune of *London Bridge Is Falling Down.*
Stamford bridge is falling down,
Falling down,
Falling down,
Stamford bridge is falling down,
Poor old Chelsea,
Build it up in claret and blue,
Claret and blue,
Claret and blue,
Build it up in claret and blue,
Poor old Chelsea.

BLUE FLAG

Sung by Blackburn Rovers.
Forever and ever,
We'll follow our team,
We're Blackburn Rovers,
We are supreme,
We'll never be mastered,
By Burnley b******s,
We'll keep the blue flag, flyin' high.

SHE WORE

Sung about David Pleat whilst at Tottenham Hotspurs.
She wore,
She wore fishnet stockings,
She wore fishnet stockings and and a wonderbra,
And when I asked,
Her why she wore the stockings,
She said she was a hooker and her client's David Pleat.

MARY POPPINS HATES WEST HAM

Sung by Leyton Orient to the tune of *Chim-chimeny* from the film *Mary Poppins*.
Chim-Chimeny,
Chim-Chimeny,
Chim-Chim Cahroo,
We hate those b******ds in claret and blue!

ONLY A POOR LITTLE SPIRITE

Sung by Mansfield Town fans to Chesterfield fans.
He's only a poor little spirite, his face was all tater'd and torn, he made me feel sick so I hit him with a brick and now he don't sing any more.

ONE MAN WENT TO MOW

One man went to mow,
Went to mow a meadow,
One man and his dog (Spot),
Went to mow a meadow.

Two men went to mow,
Went to mow a meadow,
Two men and their dog (Spot),
Went to mow a meadow.
(Repeat for up to ten men)

SHE'S FOOTBALL CRAZY

To the tune of *Football Crazy* and sung
by Bob Mortimer on *Shooting Stars*.
She's football crazy,
She's football mad,
I can't name a footballer
Ulrika's never had.

ARE YOU LISTENING?

Sung by Derby County to the tune of
Winter Wonderland.
Nottingham are you listening,
To the songs that we're singing,
Walking along, singing a song,
S******g on the Forest as we go.

SHOLA AMEOBI

To the tune of *Hokey Kokey* and sung by
Newcastle United.
You put your left foot in,
Your left foot out,
In out, in out and shake it all about,
You do the Ameobi and you turn around,
That's what it's all about!
Hey Shola Ameobi, Hey Shola Ameobi,
Hey Shola Ameobi, Knees bent Arms
Stretched, Ra Ra Ra.

FOLLOWING FOREST

Sung by Nottingham Forest to the tune
of *Mull of Kintyre*.
Far have we travelled and much have we seen,
Goodison, Anfield are places we've been,
Maine Road, Old Trafford still echo to the
sounds, of the boys in the Red shirts
from the City Ground.

THE REF HAS GOT SIX TOES

To the Tune of Is Full Of Sh*t.
The referee, has got six toes,
The referee, has got six toes,
And his mother is his sister,
The referee has got six toes.

The pictures in this book were provided courtesy of the following:
Getty Images
101 Bayham Street, London, NW1 0AG

The Cartoons in this book were provided courtesy of:
Steve Gammond and Pete Neame

Book design and artwork by Kevin Gardner,
based on an original design by Nicole Saward

Published by Green Umbrella

Series Editors Jules Gammond, Tim Exell, Vanessa Gardner

Compiled and Written by Vanessa Gardner